Folly Beach

Also by Steven Harvey

ESSAY COLLECTIONS

A Geometry of Lilies
Lost in Translation
Bound for Shady Grove

MEMOIR

The Book of Knowledge and Wonder

ANTHOLOGY

In a Dark Wood: Personal Essays by Men on Middle Age

Folly Beach

*An Essay on Family, Fear,
Physics, Philosophy & Fun*

Steven Harvey

Post-Script Press

Post-Script Press
Blairsville, Georgia

for my grandchildren

And we, who have always thought of joy
as *rising*, would feel the emotion
that almost amazes us
when a happy thing *falls*.

—Rainer Maria Rilke

One

RUNNING ACROSS THE DECK, the screen door slamming behind her, Maddie, the most imaginative of my grandchildren, joins me. She has vivid night terrors and sometimes wakes up screaming and cannot be calmed down, but today there is none of that as she skips down the boardwalk toward the music. She is five. She wears a pink nightgown with large white polka dots and hearts. "New York," "London," and "Paris" are written in script across the front of her gown beside a drawing of the Eifel Tower, and at her collar, tipped at a jaunty angle, is a small, black-and-white drawing of a checked bowtie.

Her cheeks and forehead glow with the bronze tint of early morning sun at the beach, and her hair, gloriously wild waves of auburn, blows across her face from the sea breeze.

I'm in the Crow's Nest, the widening in a wooden walkway raised aloft on pilings that runs from our rental at Folly Beach to the water, where I like to watch the sun rise. Earlier this morning before Maddie arrived I unpacked my ukulele in darkness, and saw Venus and a sliver of moon glow above the seamless, backlit curvature of the earth. Holding the ukulele to my ear, I plucked each string to check the tuning. Waves beat against sand in the half-light, and I strummed, the plunk barely audible above the surf, my fingers working their way up to second position seeking fresh chords for my melody, as the skyline suddenly ignited and incandescent cirrus clouds tilted toward the source of the light like a fleet of catamarans on their way to a regatta.

The song was "Here Comes the Sun."

Maddie running toward me has for now taken the place of the sun, and when she gets close she slows down, suddenly shy, sidles up coyly, watching me with large, brown eyes, and frowns.

What's the matter, Maddie?

She tilts her head, perplexed. Over her shoulder a black wedge of ocean points to a dark house with a cupola roof and a single window lit yellow.

To dispel the momentary gloom, I switch tunes, playing "Ukulele Lady" and singing lines like "where the tricky wicky wackies woo," Maddie watching my eyes all the while, and when I get to the part about kissing the lady, she suddenly laughs, embarrassed, breaks into a spontaneous dance, swirls with arms extended, and dashes down the length of the boardwalk, sending the crow perched on the PVC-pipe of a jerry-rigged shower flapping away toward the next house with a raucous caw.

~ ~ ~

What's the matter, Maddie?

What *is* the matter? The girl acting coy as she whirls before me matters, her chestnut hair floating at her shoulders. And the time she took skipping down the boardwalk. And the time she spent wavering before me as she stopped to listen.

And the frown.

And her pink nightgown with a small, black-and-white drawing of a checked bowtie tipped at a jaunty angle.

The wide expanse of beach and hummocks of sand—they matter. And seaweed at the water line and a far jetty slowly taking shape at sunrise as I play. *And* and *and* and *and* and *and*. Fading Venus. The rising sun. Windows aflame. The egg-shell blue sky.

These matters add up.

Ocean waves that beat against sand like slow and heavy breathing, over and over. And the screen door that opens on all this glory and slams shut like a gunshot. It matters. And the other door—the downstairs doorway. It matters too, though I'm getting ahead of myself.

And the jerry-rigged shower and the crow. Don't leave *that* out.

Matter as noun. Matter as verb.

Shifting from the concrete to the abstract and hitting all the stages in between.

These are pressing matters that can't be ignored.

The night terrors matter, I know. I saw them once, Maddie in her nightgown sitting up in bed her fingers splayed on the blankets, still asleep but screaming with

3

her eyes wide open, and Nessa, my daughter, nearby soothing her without waking her, whispering her name and shushing her and saying "I'm here," Maddie rocking back and forth, her eyes looking dead, hollering for her mother who is right in front of her smoothing her hair and pulling the tangle of loose curls away from her face and talking to her softly.

The softness matters. And the terror.

The soothing matters.

"Where the tricky wicky wackies woo" matters, too. And, of course, the kiss.

And a mind that out of habit compares sunlit clouds to catamarans floating toward the horizon dragging an ocean of beauty behind.

What I am beginning to understand this summer at age sixty five when I spend most of my time strumming my ukulele is that it all matters.

And I'm waving goodbye.

~ ~ ~

The uke has a nutty sound. When I strum it I hear the tap of coconuts under the chords, a clucking that is rich and sweet and silly at once. It's the koa wood: golden, slightly iridescent, tightly grained tone wood from Hawaii. It's the strum. It's the attack of the fingers and snap of the string. Who knows? Explaining the sound is a bit like holding the sun between your thumb and index. You can't quite put your finger on it.

Pythagoras heard numbers, not coconut shells, inside his music and speculated that numbers were behind the entire created universe. *Down, down-up down,*

down-up down goes the strumming hand over and over in a binary sequence as the melody line threads its way through a pattern of chords, and when I play a refrain I repeat the pattern, never exactly but with enough precision to fool the sensuous ear, and in time here comes the sun rising before me, creating in turn ocean and sand and wild waves of auburn hair as well as a crow in silhouette. *Down, down-up down, down-up down*—over and over in myriad variations. Sunrise. Sea. Folly Beach. Maddie dancing. The crow that unfurls its wings and floats into the next yard.

Nothing more than the physical embodiment of numbers?

The nuttiness of numbers?

I hear coconuts.

~ ~ ~

"Scoop up a handful of sand on Folly Beach," Stratton Lawrence writes in *Images of America: Folly Beach*, "and you are literally holding the mountains in your hands." For millions of years the Appalachian range where I live slowly eroded depositing sediment along the South Carolina coast, creating beaches like Folly.

When Maddie as a toddler visited me at our house in the Georgia mountains, she liked to play with stones in the gravel path and would hold up her dirty hands. "Here's how you take care of that," I told her, smacking my hands together and brushing them back and forth. I held up both hands for Maddie to see. "That's *that!*" She followed suit, standing in the gravel and brushing her hands together.

"That's *that!*"

And we laughed when she held up her palms.

At the beach, I pick up a handful of notes in the morning and cup them in my hand and as they ooze through my fingers I see mica and granite and silica that has drifted here from my mountain home, all of where I live eventually washing down to this spot, and, giving up the banjo for the ukulele, I'm lost in the abundance of this *now*, which is all I'm entitled to. I get the notes I pluck, but each time I lay my palm against the full set of strings to silence them, my hand comes up empty.

Down, down-up, down, down, and *down.*

"That's *that!*"

~ ~ ~

The word "folly" can be traced back to the word for "blow." It is also the root of the English word for "bellows" and eventually, by following the principle of sound correspondences which replaces the "b" with an "f", the root branched off into words such as "fool" and "folly." A variation of the root word means "to thrive" which we hear in "blossom" and "bloom" and, by a similar consonant shift, in the word "foliage". So, the primary definition of the word "folly" may mean a life without purpose or meaning, but it thrives in the same etymological bed as the word for "flower." Folly Beach got its name because of the heavy foliage that covered the island. "The first English settlers," Lawrence explains, "used the Old English term 'Folly' to label islands with dense foliage. Only on present-day Folly Beach did the name stick."

Folly Beach, the beach in full bloom.

~ ~ ~

My son Sam is in charge of the cheese grits at the beach. He finds a deep pot and fills it and while waiting for the water to boil gathers up the other ingredients: cheddar cheese, butter, and salt. He is an informal morning chef, dressed in a t-shirt and loose pajama bottoms, his blond hair slightly tousled. The biggest of all of the Harveys, he fills up the space as he leans over the stove, reading package labels, and scratching his head with the handle of the large serving spoon. The kitchen has a Formica counter that wraps around three sides. It opens out on the living room making a small breakfast bar that the kids use every morning.

"Good morning, Mr. Penguin," Sam says when Owen walks into the room and climbs up a stool.

The name fits. My grandson Owen is a compact boy and there is a slight waddle as he walks, his feet, which even his mother admits are pretty big for a boy his size, kicked out on either side. He speaks in a very careful and clear voice and carries himself with a slight formality, as if he were wearing a suit. When he was still in diapers he loved to push kitchen chairs around a room for no reason at all with an air of deliberation and purpose that you might expect of a constable doing his rounds. Even here on a barstool eating Gorilla Munch beside his cousin Maddie who likes to lean back in her chair and talk with her hands, he sits erect and still and says "please" when he asks for something.

7

"Grandpa, would you please take us to the downstairs doorway tomorrow?"

The beach house is on a stilted platform and the entranceway from the street is through a small door downstairs in a darkened hallway.

I look up as Owen's mom, Angie, enters the room just waking up.

"Owen's concept of time is elastic," she says covering up a yawn. "He means soon. He may mean *any* time."

I nod. "How about after breakfast, O," and he smiles.

Maddie announces that she likes the cartoon "Sleepwalking'" because Goofy "goes zip into the wall," and, as she laughs a very exaggerated and false laugh, I smile at my own childhood memory of a cut out profile of Goofy running a marathon through walls in his sleep with Mickey chasing after him. There's Goofy running down the street. And there's the empty space in the shape of Goofy in one wall after another behind him as if nothing's the matter.

Nothing's the matter.

That's the joke.

~ ~ ~

The ukulele is also a joke. The word means "jumping flea" in Hawaiian, and the most common response when I pull mine out of the case is laughter.

It is so tiny. Mine is about the size of my forearm and weighs almost nothing. The fretboard—where half of the work of the ukulele happens—is about seven inches long, and the fingers are jumping like fleas in part to keep from getting tangled up. The other hand strums, often sounding several times with each swipe, creating rich counter-rhythms and a fullness of sound all from a box that you can tuck inside a pillowcase. The ukulele is intensity created by compression. Exhilaration within limits. A tightly wound boundlessness.

"You get all that sound out of *there*?"

That's the joke.

The little bang.

~ ~ ~

There are jokes and there are jokes.

"They're putting *milk* in their *co*ffee," Maddie says with exaggerated irony watching bleary-eyed adults stirring cups and mugs. Owen's daddy, my son Matt, is up, and my wife, Barbara, is beginning to stir in our bedroom.

Anna—the three-year-old cousin of Owen and Maddie—shouts "Anna do it!" when her mother, Sam's wife Brooke, tries to pull up the girl's bathing suit. Anna fidgets and crosses her arms with a frown. Brooke shakes her head and throws her arms up exasperated at Anna's stubbornness, walking back into the bedroom to change baby Caroline, leaving Anna half dressed.

Maddie and Owen in stage whispers start listing other ingredients that might go into a coffee cup.

"Orange juice," Maddie whispers, giggling.

Owen cups his hand as if telling her a secret in a stage whisper. He doesn't really have a handle on duplicity yet since he cups his hand the wrong way when he whispers, including me in the conversation rather than keeping me out.

"Poop!" he whispers loudly.

"A cow!" Maddie says in full voice slapping her hands on the countertop.

Then with outsized gestures, she begins taking the ingredients out of the imaginary cup one at a time, making a face with each one.

"Anna do it!" her cousin chimes in, sidling up to the bar like a moll, her bathing suit awry.

~   ~   ~

It is only natural, I suppose, given the name of our beach, that my mind should turn to architectural follies, those buildings "constructed primarily for decoration," but looking as though they had "some other purpose," I discover, checking my phone, shading the screen with my hand. I know that Wikipedia, the source of this bit of information, is not entirely reliable and even the Wiki editors warn that the article "needs additional citations for verification," but I'm at the beach and, anyway, as I look at the photographs of follies from around the world, I sense that the writer got it about right: a folly is an illusion built to please.

A folly can appear "to be so extravagant that it transcends the range of garden ornaments usually associated with the class of buildings to which it belongs." Extravagant, yes, wandering outside the boundaries. I like the anonymous writer's way around the subject, especially when he cites the Oxford English Dictionary which notes that the word "folly" began as "a popular name for any costly structure considered to have shown folly in the builder."

He offers the example of "Beckford's Folly" which he describes as "an extremely expensive early Gothic Revival country house that collapsed under the weight of its tower." Certainly the photographs of other examples in the article say it all: The "Dunmore Pineapple" in Scotland with its ridiculously magnificent topknot in the shape of the fruit, Hagley Castle built by Lord Lyttleton to look like a "small ruined medieval castle," and The Swallow's Nest, a miniature castle of

stone perched on a craggy outcropping overlooking the Cape of Ai-Todor in Crimea.

"They have no purpose other than as ornament," Wikipedia adds, and there is "often an element of fakery in their construction." They were "built or commissioned for pleasure."

I think of The Crow's Nest, my early morning perch, the ornamental widening of the walkway to the beach that holds our family every evening while we are here.

And the dark house with a cupola roof and a single window lit yellow at dawn.

And the sand castle that we built, a useless defense against forces that sweep us away.

"We could decorate the walls with shells," Barbara said, while we lay baking in the midday sun, but that was later. I'm getting ahead of myself again.

~ ~ ~

"Getting ahead of myself" is an interesting phrase. It's a bit like getting lost except that you find yourself, willy-nilly, further up the path.

Nothing lost but the way and the now and, I suppose, the losing.

Sometimes my life feels like the crumbling ruins of an abandoned fort and sometimes like a miniature castle of stone perched on a craggy outcropping overlooking the Cape of Ai-Todor in Crimea, but not *now*, not this moment when Sam is stirring the grits and Maddie is pulling the universe out of a cup of coffee.

I've been getting ahead of myself a lot since I retired, a dangerous impatience. My self is the one person I don't want to get ahead of, right?

I mean, we all know where this is headed.

~ ~ ~

Wearing her footed pajamas with the sun, moon, and star designs on it, Caroline, who is Sam and Brook's five-month-old daughter and my youngest grandchild, lies on a pink blanket on the wood floors of the main room while we step around her getting ready for the beach.

"Look at Caroline turn over," I say, sitting on the sofa across from her waiting for Barbara to lather my back in sunscreen.

The baby puts her foot in her mouth and leans onto her shoulder using her head, her largest feature, to pull her forward. Several of us have stopped what we are doing to watch, as she strains to roll over, defying gravity it seems with her head and toes way over the edge of the blanket. "You can do it!" we tell her as she pushes a little harder, but she doesn't quite make it and tumbles back again smiling and kicking her feet. Brooke walks by, laughing. She's seen all of this before many times. The rest of us keep cheering Caroline on—a small cluster of adults gathering—as the baby, foot in mouth, leans onto her shoulder to try again.

"Anna do it," Anna says. At three, she can get jealous of the attention going to the baby. She lies beside her sister on the floor in her swim suit, puts her foot in her mouth and easily turns over and walks off, self-satisfied. Maddie, who is five, lies down next, and starts to put her foot in her mouth, her mother Nessa rolling her eyes, but the rest of us have turned our attention back to baby Caroline by then who is pumping her arms and smiling broadly at the older kids, and Maddie, glancing around the room takes in the situation and thinks better of rolling over—suddenly embarrassed, aware that she is acting a little stupid. Quickly she stands, crosses her arms and backs off whispering, "I can do it too."

She joins us on the adult side of the blanket, looking in.

~ ~ ~

Defying gravity. It may be the best definition of folly. Imagine a beach full of people who feel suddenly light, no, weightless, opening their arms and floating upward, giving in to their first impulse to laugh before becoming terrified.

Two

IN THE MORNING at low tide I haul chairs and umbrellas from the boardwalk to the beach. I usually mount the umbrellas at the high-tide water mark, screwing the plastic bases into the sand and lowering umbrella shafts into position. I open two or three chairs there too. The rest of the chairs I drag to the low-tide water line where I sit before the family arrives.

Alone for now I look out at the ocean and imagine a seafloor littered with creatures. I remember an illustration from *Ocean Planet* and later when I take the book down from the shelves I discover that the names and appearances of the creatures are nightmarish and even stranger than I imagined: red-capped vampire squid, coffin fish, spiky sea urchins, angler fish with terrifying maws all spread at random on the sea floor, star-faced sea slugs in rainbow colors, the fanged vampire fish with its hinged lower jaw, toxic sea cucumbers, bioluminescent black dragon fish, stargazers with eyes atop their skulls, toothy moray eels, coral red sea robins. In my mind I see the entire menagerie lined up in rows, like vacationers in Atlantic City, slowly moving forward.

I stand at the lapping edge of everything as water creeps between my toes. Something's coming my way.

~ ~ ~

At mid-morning the rest of the family hits the sand and sprawls: six beach chairs, two umbrellas, four or five bags of towels and diapers, a pile of plastic buckets and shovels and sand molds of various shapes and sizes, and a "Baby Pop Up Beach Tent" for Caroline. Maddie and her Uncle Sam head for the ocean to hop waves, holding hands as they make their way across the wide expanse of sand. Hesitant to take on the breakers, Owen hangs back. He plays alone with the sand toys for a while, dons sunglasses and flops into a beach chair, gets bored, and heads back to the house.

Brooke and Nessa follow Anna, who walks belly first with a purposeful stride to the water's edge, and I'm in charge of baby Caroline. Brooke has spread a blanket and pillows in the tent to hem her baby in and, as I lean in the opening Caroline looks about, alert and happy, shaking her fists and kicking the air. She wears a single-piece pink bathing suit with hearts and monkey faces on it. She has tossed a bottle of breast-milk off to one side and has not yet realized it is out of her hand.

I'm in black swim trunks and a faded t-shirt that has ukuleles in a tropical Hawaiian scene printed on it. Beneath the scene is a caption in script: "Enchanted Sounds of Our Heritage." I unzip my beach ukulele, a purple one with a plastic body, and begin to play

"Carolina Moon," a song with her name in it, but Caroline looks away from me, at her empty hand and slowly realizing the bottle is gone begins to cry. I put the pacifier in her mouth, but she spits it out. I hand her the bottle but she tosses it aside. I try to finish the song but she's wailing, kicking the air hard, her face turning red as she squints into the glare above us.

Another fickle fan.

I step back while reinforcements arrive in the form of Brooke and Nessa, mother and aunt. I look at the wide beach—the blank margin—where there is no script and nothing can hide.

~ ~ ~

Folly Beach. Folly blaze. Folly incandescent. Folly illuminate. The burning edge as the sun rises high above the water. Brooke's blonde hair a-flame. The beach sand a-shimmer. Caroline's sun bonnet tossing plates of white into the air.

That's the other lost meaning of the word "folly": "to shine, flash, burn" and "shining white and various bright colors" and "fire." The meaning is hidden in our words for 'blond' and 'bleach' and 'blaze' and 'blink'.

Folly sets a torch to the sand on summer afternoons searing feet. Like a forest fire it burns away from a scorched center. Like our dying sun it leaves behind a black hole. It casts long, hard shadows and swipes a red-hot thumbprint on Matt's stomach where he missed a spot.

~ ~ ~

Now that I'm retired, I've begun having private conversations with the authors I taught, a kind of career wrap up. I lie on the beach, slathered up in sunscreen with my ball cap pulled down over my eyes and who strolls my way but Lao Tzu. Well that's not exactly right since no one knows who Lao Tzu is. The name itself means "old boy" which is a pretty common phrase in the mountains for a character who gets away with something. "That old boy walked out with a bottle under his coat." So I picture Lao Tzu as an old man with a moonshine twinkle in his eye.

It is fitting that he appears to me here because he thought that the best way to live is to be like water which yields and overpowers at once. The "sea pronounces something, over and over, in a hoarse whisper; I cannot quite make it out," Annie Dillard writes in *Teaching a Stone to Talk*, but Lao Tzu knew the language of water and under the shadow of my Folly Beach cap, I think I've got it, too.

"Yield and overpower," the waves say. "Yield and overpower."

Over and over.

Unfortunately, it is not always easy to make out what Lao Tzu's book, *The Tao Te Ching,* is saying. In class I used Jonathan Star's "Verbatim Translation" which gives every possible English rendering of each word in the text. The word "Tao" for instance can mean "Tao, The Tao, way, path, paths, That, 'The Absolute', or 'Nature.'" "Te" can mean "obtain, gain, possess, benefit, receive, get, or attain." And "Ching" can mean "By-paths, side roads, deviations, or sidetracked." So I

18

asked the students to choose their own combination of words to create a customized translation of verse one of the Tao. Their own Tao. The possibilities were mind-boggling.

Some translations of the first line were sobering: "The Tao that can be told is not the eternal Tao." Others were concrete: "The path that becomes trodden is surely not the fixed path." A few produced abstract gobbledygook: "The Absolute that can be spoken of is not identical with the everlasting Absolute."

I groaned at that last one, throwing my hands in the air.

"*That* way is not *the* way!"

So much for verse one.

Not long after my classes on Lao Tzu, I translated verse two of the Tao and it spoke clearly to me: "Work done?" it asked. "Retire, naturally, and the results last forever."

~   ~   ~

Yield and overpower. And yield. And yield.

~   ~   ~

The 17th century Japanese poet Bashō was another one of the writers who taught me how to let go of my last year of college teaching. In *Narrow Road to the Interior* he compared his life to a boat adrift in which "every day is a journey, and the journey itself is home." In May of 1689, when the fields were misty in the morning, he found himself distracted by thoughts of travel. He busied himself by mending his travel clothes and rubbing powder on his legs to strengthen them for walking. He turned over his duties at school to his former students, arranged for others to look after his house, and started off on the journeys that would preoccupy him for the last five years of his life.

On the day of his departure he left a poem on his door. "Even this grass hut," he wrote in the Sam Hamill translation, "may be transformed/ into a doll's house."

I remember closing the pages over my thumb after I dismissed the class and gazing out of the bank of windows at the sunlit parking lot as students carrying books floated through the shimmer above car hoods.

"Yes," I thought, "a doll's house."

~   ~   ~

"Think of mixing cream into coffee," the physicist Sean Carroll writes in *The Big Picture*. In the beginning, when the cream and coffee are separate, entropy is low, and in the end, when they have mixed together to form one new thing, it is low as well. But between those times—when the cream splashes into the coffee before it is stirred with a spoon—lovely, complex structures form. "Tendrils of cream reach into the coffee in intricate and beautiful ways." The contents of the cup for the moment look like a swirling Milky Way.

"Entropy goes up," as the second law of thermodynamics says it should, explains Carroll, "but complexity first goes up, then goes down." We live in a young universe that exhibits medium entropy and is highly complex. "The initially smooth configuration has become increasingly lumpy over the last several billion years as tiny perturbations in the density of matter have grown into planets, stars, and galaxies."

And into chestnut hair and foam-tipped waves and the single yellow eye of the crow and iridescent cirrus clouds appearing to tilt toward the sun and the illusion of a black-and-white checked bowtie embossed on threads of cotton linen. Increasing complexity is alluring, the modifying phrases of our lives growing longer and longer, complicating matters, as the paragraph peters out. The days don't just add up; they twist back on themselves like strands of DNA.

I pour a jigger of bourbon and watch the nearly transparent swirls of ice melting into the liquor. "Stop just shy of the brim," Lao Tzu writes in verse nine, "without sloshing over." I hold the glass up to my eyes saluting folly and gaze into the swirl.

The universe ablaze.

The universe in full bloom.

When I bring the drink to my lips, it tastes sweet.

~　~　~

I weave thoughts and memories so that they play upon each other like the ingredients in a recipe or the dance of electrons in a chemistry experiment, the combination creating something new. I risk ruining the cake and blowing up the laboratory as I keep adding, but I can't seem to help myself. Maddie bounds across the boardwalk, her hair and face catching morning fire, and I see that the sun deserves a section as does the ukulele she is skipping to which causes me to think of my banjo back home in the mountains and the sand of the Appalachian hills draining down over eons of time until it reaches the Folly shoreline. And this and this and this—an endless polysyndeton suggesting the cornucopia of an ordinary morning, so I push on happily.

And there's something else. The ingredients in the cake change each other when mixed, and the chemicals are transformed in the experiment into lovely combinations I can't resist. Add this to that and this alters that and this and that alter that and that and that, the mix suggesting sex and relationships and family resemblances. Sam's smile as he serves up grits wears the glow of sunlit Appalachian sand and the nuttiness of the ukulele and the gaiety of Maddie disbursing crows by waving her arms in the air as she dances to the end of the pier. All is transformed in the mixing. Anna's glance back at me, as she heads down to the beach belly first, wears the sunshine of the sun and the "You Are My Sunshine" of her favorite song, and her blonde hair floats above her shoulder in the sea breeze like the pelicans hovering high overhead.

~ ~ ~

Secretly, I love Wikipedia—a sad admission for a college professor to make, but heck, I'm no longer a professor. Wikipedia describes itself as "The Free Encyclopedia" that is "the largest and most popular general reference work on the World Wide Web," but that is not why I love it. It is open sourced, meaning that those "who access the site can edit most of its articles," but that is not why I love it either.

My love for the site has nothing to do with its accuracy which approaches that of the world's great encyclopedias such as the *Britannica*, nor do I begrudge it the occasional inaccuracy such as the intentional insertion of false material on John Seigenthaler in May 2005 which created a scandal. I don't confuse Wikipedia, or any encyclopedia, with peer-reviewed scholarly journals. I know it's *not* definitive—it doesn't pretend to be—and I'm glad it is not a scholarly journal.

The entries are not necessarily written by experts but by those who are passionate about their subjects and they are corrected by its readers, a concept that I like very much, but that is not why I love Wikipedia.

No, there's something else. I walk out to the Crow's Nest alone on a clear night and see the stars spangle the black sky of an expanding universe and the moonlight spill my way like glittering silverware across a wide ocean curved at the faintly lit horizon. The edges moving toward me and away from me keep remaking themselves. The ocean pounds the shore, but the tides reach their level simply by finding it, as the wave sweeps across the sand, changing all that it touches.

It is the groping nature of Wikipedia that lures me in. It's itchiness. The ambition to map out a pattern bigger than any of us can understand. That is what I love about Wikipedia. About all of Cyberspace. Its *lack* of definition. The way it forever resists having the last word.

~ ~ ~

The last word, yes. That's the matter.

~ ~ ~

"Follies come from money and security and peace," writes Barbara Jones in *Follies & Grottoes,* a lovely, old book with torn, reddish-brown hard covers packed with information about follies accompanied by black-and-white photos and deft line drawings by the author, first published in 1953. According to Jones, when we have enough "money and security and peace" we apparently create useless buildings and dig holes in the earth that go nowhere, their futility a testament to the human urge to create as if nothing else matters. They are playthings for rich men.

Take Sir Francis Dashwood. In the eighteenth century he built the Hell-Fire Follies on his estate at West Wycombe. It was, in fact, a small village of follies, many of them now destroyed, that includes a golden ball draped in chains overlooking a graveyard, a temple to Daphne that is a façade, flint buildings with pyramid-capped corners, a cottage built tall like a skyscraper, fake ruins, a sham church tower three stories high "with buttresses and flanking piers and four white pinnacles," and a toy church "with a lovely model quality as if printed on a large sheet of cardboard." It gives a nod toward antiquity: the Hell Fire Caves, a "quarter mile of tunnel" that leads to the "Catacombs of Rome" and "the big Banquet Hall with four Monks Cells, and finally the Inner Temple." It also looks ahead toward the future. At one time, the gardens had been laid out in the shape of a naked woman visible only from above, "every walk and wood and clump of trees dedicated to a joke that could not have been truly enjoyed till the invention of the aeroplane."

More foolish than the buildings and grounds were the legendary goings on in the Hell Fire Club where the Order of Saint Francis of Medmenham met twice a year led by Hell-Fire Francis himself. These members of the nobility conducted "mild revels, celebrating the black mass on desecrated altars, eating strange food served at 100 feet above or below the earth, drinking wine poured by naked girls and looking at the portraits of the Kings of England which hung above the long drinking sofas in the Chapter house." At the conclusion of one event a partier dressed up as a baboon with horns to simulate the devil pulled a cord to release a real-life ape that hopped "on to the shoulder of Lord Sandwich." Later when the parties were moved to West Wycombe, Sir Francis' revelers assigned a jury of aristocrats to determine the sex of the Chevalier d'Eon de Beaumont that "could only arrive at a verdict of Doubtful."

It is hard to disagree with Jones' conclusion: "They were rich, and childish men; they were bored." In place of purpose they built follies.

~ ~ ~

But what is wrong with creating a Temple of Diana, a Temple of Music, and a Temple of the Winds at West Wycombe Park? Who cares if Hell-Fire Francis and these other old fops were bored? Some of these follies, the by-products of "money and security and peace," attain a serenity that seems inseparable from their uselessness. The Temple of Apollo—which has no clear purpose, serving sometimes as a gate and at other times as an arena for cockfighting—wastes most of its days looking merely pretty as it peers modestly from behind tall hedges, its gray and rough stone parapets in startling contrast with the softer lines of its arch, the delicate geometric shapes of the ceiling tiles, and the warm reddish tones of the cloister walls within. It blends into a landscape of unusual and exotic plants and trees that Horace Walpole in his *History of the Modern Taste in Gardening* claimed lends a "richness of colouring so peculiar to the modern landscape," peculiar here meaning appropriate, fitting. Creating a party site inspired by the Temple of Vesta in Rome certainly beats going to war which was the other hobby of European aristocrats.

What do humans do when hunger, violence, sexual gratification, and the accumulation of wealth and power no longer matter, I wonder as I sit in a rented beach chair next to Barbara in the first year of my retirement looking out on the ocean, an unread book in my lap? Out of nowhere two well-fed little boys dragging large, industrial style shovels with yellow shafts and tempered blades walk in circles around our spot wordlessly dragging the shovels behind them. They are making some sort of serendipitous shape with one rule: to avoid hitting any of the rest of us with our exposed and vulnerable toes extended into the beach sand. The boys' paths crisscross each other as the furrowed lines become more elaborately intertwined, their design being left to impulse rather than will. One marches toward the ocean—they are moving fast but not running—and the other heads off to our left for a while extending their structure, but soon they are back creating a tighter frame for us. A drawing? A filigree? A briar patch?

A tightly wound boundlessness?

A Temple of Sand?

Suddenly they stop and lean back against their shovels casting their eyes lovingly over their creation, smiling as if to say "that's *that*."

A phalanx of pelicans floats overhead, their shadows rippling over lines drawn in the sand.

~ ~ ~

This is the summer of the horseshoe crab. Their carcasses are everywhere along the beach. Most are just empty shells. Barbara and I come upon several on our walk and stop to look at one. It is a copper-colored hard shell—only the upper half—with a squared off notch where the lower section should be, the carapace rising to a median ridge and two lesser lateral ridges that rise to hard knots.

"Their eyes are fake," I say, poking at the shell with my toe. Thinking that like the morphogenesis of fake eyes in butterflies or peacocks these hard knobs on the shell were simply to ward off predators. Not true. Those eyes are real, I found out later after a quick check on my phone, and a horseshoe crab uses them and other eyes located all over its body to find a mate.

But the eyes in this one are gone, and, with the bottom half missing, it looks like a mask gazing back at us emptily with a message as monotonous as the waves of the sea.

"I am ancient," the carapace says as we stand beside it, our long, white legs naked and exposed. "Prehistoric. Hard on the outside and soft within. I will outlive you and your kind."

~ ~ ~

Folly Beach was named "Coffin Land" on a map of James Island and the Charleston area published in 1780. Shipwrecks were common and the island was a quarantine site for those suffering from plague and cholera. Often the sick were dropped off at the beach before the ships reached port in Charleston. "Survivors," Stratton Lawrence explains, "were picked up on the way back to sea." At times, shipwreck and illness came together, compounding suffering and death. *The Amelia*, a ship following the coastline and bound for New Orleans, wrecked on the contaminated shores of the island, and twenty of the one hundred and twenty passengers died in the subsequent outbreak of cholera.

The original inhabitants, most likely a Bohicket tribe of Cusabo Indians, were long gone when Charles Towne was established by the English in 1670. "There remains," Lieutenant Governor William Bull wrote in 1770, "nothing of them but their names." Engravings by the explorer Jacques LeMoyne show the Cusabo killing alligators by jamming long poles into their mouths while beating them with clubs and roasting fish on a raised wooden frame over a blazing fire. Other early inhabitants of the island included pirates, like "Edward 'Blackbeard' Teach and Stede Bonnet, known as the Gentleman Pirate," Stratton writes, "who preyed on merchant ships sailing past the island in 1717 and 1718," the buccaneer history leading to rumors of ghosts and hidden treasure at Folly.

Taking a morning break from the beach, I sit in the Crow's Nest writing while pelicans in gaunt patrol above me set their wings. They once floated along the shoreline of Coffin Land and now, like the tildes below each section of my story, they haunt my text, coming and going as they please, but while they are here they hover ominously, reading currents, conserving energy, relentlessly hunting down life. When they spot their prey, they tumble for the kill, wings tilted, swastikas against bright blue.

"We are all treasure hunters," I write. "Haunted by ghosts." I draw a line beneath my words and make a dot before closing my small book.

Three

THE HARVEY FAMILIES converged on Folly from several directions on Saturday, June 21, 2014. Matt, Angie, and Owen, the "Wise" Harveys from Wise, Virginia, had the longest drive from their home in the mountains not far from the West Virginia border. Nessa and Maddie had the shortest trip from Athens, Georgia. Barbara and I spent the night in Charleston, just south of the beach, so that we could arrive early and set up the house a bit. The young Harveys—Sam, Brooke, Anna, and Caroline—had a shorter trip than Sam's older brother, Matt, but it probably seemed the longest, with two children under four in the car, especially along the stretch of I-26 south near Columbia where traffic often comes to a stop on summer weekends, car hoods rippling the steamy air.

Barbara and I arrived at Avocet, the real estate agency that organized the rental of the house, ahead of the others. The policy there was that the keys could not be given out until two in the afternoon, and even at one o'clock several families were milling about in the lobby waiting, so Barbara and I left to get groceries and supplies. As we drove out, we passed Sam's car heading in and Barbara called Brooke on her cell phone to explain that they could pick up the key at Avocet and open the house. We would meet them after we finished at the store. In the background we could hear babies in pandemonium.

"We're going crazy," Brooke said, laughing anxiously.

Barbara cast a knowing, sidelong look my way when she clicked off the phone.

The young Harveys' car pulled up to the agency at twelve minutes before two, and when Sam came back to the car from the desk to explain that they had to wait, Brooke, who is about five feet tall, marched past the families that were clustered in the crowded lobby and cast a baleful eye on the pretty, young clerk. "I have two screaming babies in the car," she said, holding out her hand. "I need those keys now!"

~ ~ ~

Sometimes time does not seem elastic. It is the time of waiting, the time of the dull job when you have nothing better to do than stare as the second hand of the clock makes its inexorable round. It is the time of the bad day. The time of one damned thing after another. The Ancient Greeks has a name for this time, I used to tell my students. They called it *Kronos*. The time of the chronometer. The time of screaming babies when all anyone wants is for the time to end.

But the Greeks, in their wisdom, had another name for time taken from a different deity in the pantheon, *Kairos. Kairos* is the time of the seasons, each different from the last. When we are experiencing *Kairos,* time is elastic, and we can live in a moment forever. Writers savor such time. It is the time of the lyric poem. The time of childhood when the hours run honey slow. It is Owen's time, the time of the downstairs doorway.

"When you look back on your past and create a timeline with cross-hatches to mark the years," I say to my class drawing a line across the white board and hatching it quickly, "there are years of your life so bunched up in your mind that you can hardly remember them at all. They are for you the unremarkable years. But there are other years filled with memory and meaning that loom large and require a wide segment of the timeline." I skip a large space on the line and make a crosshatch, stepping back so that the students would turn their attention to the gap in the line.

"For me that's seventh grade, and we know what happens then," I say with a smile.

"*Kairos* is meaningful time. In the movies it is the time when the camera goes into slow motion as the basketball leaves the player's splayed fingers, the seams along the leather slowly spinning," I say, rotating my hands deliberately, the magic marker caught under my thumb, "while the ball rides its lazy arc descending in agonizing dreaminess with the outcome still in the balance, taking all the time in the world to float toward the hoop, until at last it drops through the basket"—I clap my hands, and turn to the class—"snapping the net in real time."

"Film makers learned that from writers." It is a time of eagerness and anxiety, torment and excitement. It is when we are having "the time of our lives."

~ ~ ~

The Crow's Nest did not always go by that name. For a while we called it "that place where we have drinks and talk while looking at the sunset." But one evening while sitting on the porch and gazing at the structure from a distance, we settle on the right phrase. Made of weathered wood, it is suspended high above the dunes and looks vaguely like something off of a pirate's ship, so we are drawn to maritime terms right away. Someone suggests "deck" and "observation deck," and I—bracing myself for snickers—offer "poop deck," not sure   exactly   what   a   poop   deck   is.

"Well," I explain defensively as Matt doubles over with laughter holding in his drink with puffed cheeks and Sam smiles and looks off into the sun. "I mean, isn't that what a poop deck is?" I say gesturing toward the thing. We all look again, Brooke shading her eyes.

From below, the pilings that dig into the beach look jerry rigged, the shifting sands creating an uncertain foundation that has been amended and added to higgledy-piggledy over the years. Above that sketchy base, the structure holds firm by the sheer accumulation of lumber and sand below and gradually acquires a greater degree of order as the eye follows the entire framework up to a walkway with slatted sides that dips slightly at one end where the steps begin. An incongruous PVC shower hangs over the deck like a microphone boom. The octagonal widening of the walkway that we are struggling to name is set apart from all of this: tapered a bit, it gentles the austerity of the narrow boardwalk and hangs above the haphazard foundation like a chalice of wood held up to the sky.

"Crow's Nest," Brooke says, smiling in the sunset light. "Let's call it the Crow's Nest."

~ ~ ~

The jigsaw puzzle this year is The Ludicrous Library, a 1500 piece headache based on a painting by Colin Thompson, a children's author and illustrator from England. The library has many rooms crammed with books and a maze of stairwells that hangs suspended in midair. I have no patience for puzzles— the pieces look alike to me—but the rest of my family

35

likes to kill time in the hot part of the day or late at night, their heads bent over the rectangular outer edge of locked pieces that extend in peninsulas and islands of color on the dining room table, their fingers poking through loose pieces outside the edge that have yet to find their slots in the whole. There is just enough success, the pleasant snap of two pieces linking up and the occasional happy discovery of odd archipelagos of related pieces, to keep the more patient members of the family—Brooke, Nessa, Matt, Barbara, and Angie—quietly entertained.

This year when I see Nessa spill the contents of the box—lining up the edge pieces off to the side and turning the rest face up—I remember my friend David who liked to sabotage the puzzlers. David has an odd sense of humor. He used to tell stories about Danny Decapitation to his children to keep them from sticking their arms and heads out of car windows. He taught college history and when the course got to Marie Antoinette, he waited until he described her beheading and bit into a blood capsule hidden in his mouth, the trickle of red running down his chin as he finished the lecture. Sometimes when he lectured he walked out of the front doorway to his classroom and back in the back doorway without missing a beat. For many years our families went to the beach together, and David liked to steal one piece from the puzzle, causing frustration and fury while everyone searched the floor and behind sofa cushions until he miraculously found the missing item in his pocket. "Here it is!" he would say with a flourish, putting the last piece in place triumphantly while the rest of us groaned.

I'm tempted to steal one myself until I look at Nessa's squint as she examines a single piece for clues and Brooke's consternated face as she fingers another piece and searches the table top for its silhouette.

Our puzzles are hard enough.

~ ~ ~

Or, maybe our puzzles are too easy. In the mornings I usually place both hands on the wide rail of the Crow's Nest and look out to the horizon where sea and sky merge. Like the ensign setting aside his spyglass, I'm gazing into a seascape so abstract and clear that it has almost no distinguishing shape at all, or at best, a cloud shape, amorphous, apparently random, and billowing grandly on nothing, like endless fingerings on a fretboard that produce variations in vibrating air. Staring into a puzzle of countless, but apparently seamless, pieces, I enter a continuum that connects me to all.

Maybe all *is* number. Maybe the number is one.

~ ~ ~

Or three. There are three Stooges, three little pigs, three wise men—and the Tresham Triangular Lodge, one of the oldest follies in England built near Rushton in Northamtonshire by Sir Thomas Tresham, a Roman Catholic imprisoned during the Reformation for refusing to become Protestant. When he was released he celebrated his freedom by creating a folly. In the photos beside the Wikipedia article that I called up on my phone I could see that the building itself is made of alternating bands of red and white limestone brick lending a muted pastel charm to the structure as the sun passes overhead and the nine spires plus a taller central spire cast gothic shadows over the lawn in the afternoon. It is boldly self-effacing—"ostentatiously incognito" as one blogger named Scriblerus put it—which may be how it escaped destruction during the

English civil wars despite its celebration of his forbidden faith.

Later at home when I examined more photos of
the building through Creative Commons on my
computer and read about it in Barbara Jones' book, I
learned more details. The three-story building has three
equal sides each of them thirty three and a third feet
long and cut at 60° angles to each other. Each side has
three, three-foot gables which are topped with
pinnacles and decorated with gargoyles. Three trefoil-
shaped windows with triangular panes at the center
illuminate the top floor while the second floor windows
are cut into the stone, each with a crucifix shape
surrounded by twelve circular openings. Three and
three and three and three—it's obsessive. Over the
heraldic shield at the three-foot south-east entrance to
the building is the Latin inscription "Tres testimonium
dant" which means "Three bears witness," but, since
Tres was Sir Thomas' nickname, it could also mean
"Tresham bears witness."

Bears witness to what?

The Trinity is the easy answer, but it is hard to gaze
at this structure on a computer screen and not suspect
that there is more going on here with Tresham's
obsession. The building invites me into its puzzle with
a spirit that is playful and grand; quiet and meditative, it
absorbs my attention and holds the eye as it leads my
gaze upward along its sharp spires and beyond itself.
The Latin inscription on the southeast wall, the one that
faces the mid-winter sunrise, is based on a verse of
scripture that says "I make Light and I make Darkness,"
and I remember Folly Beach at dawn when Venus and
the moon share a dark sky and the diagonal created by

the shoreline and the horizon point beyond the dark house with a cupola roof and a single window lit yellow to a vanishing point on the horizon.

Patrick Macdermott, writing for the "Research into Lost Knowledge Organization Trust," may be stretching the point when he writes that The Triangular Lodge bears witness to all creation and is "less a testimony in stone to the Trinity of God" than an exploration of the "occult sciences, of the 7 liberal arts and of space and of time." But who knows? Though intended as a celebration of the Trinity, the cozy triangular shapes point outward in all directions. It is, Barbara Jones writes, "a lovely essay in stone arithmetic," and may be unsurpassed among all follies "for pure conceit." The Latin inscription in the southwest wall says "I meditate on your work, Lord, and faint."

If it isn't about everything, it may be the best we can do.

~ ~ ~

The opposite of folly is the shadow it casts. The Triangular Lodge invites me to come closer—the urge is not to flee but stay, touch the cool limestone, and look up at the façade overhead decorated with "incongruous gothic flamboyant motifs," as Jones describes them, "and nice birds that lean back a little drunk." Unfolding in threes—three walls, three floors, trefoil windows, and three times three triangular spires—the lodge sheds any dour symbolic significance and seems playful like a toy, or, better, a puzzle with the pieces all intact.

All but one, the shadow it casts, opening like a freshly dug grave in the neatly trimmed lawn.

~ ~ ~

"What's *that?*" I ask as Sam shades his eyes and looks off at the tiny arc against the blue sky. Like a crow's wing, a kite appears off in the distance at dusk tacking our way from the far end of the curving beach. At first we only see the kite—taut against wind, black, ominous, and aglow—floating high back and forth in a smudgy rose sky, but eventually we make out the surfer as well, an ebony silhouette against jade water and foamy surf.

A steady, cross-shore breeze pulls the kite behind and off to one side of the surfer, but he is headed our way, gliding parallel to the beach. Sam, Barbara, Matt, and I watch as the kite grows larger and the surfer, moving his arms like a sorcerer casting a spell, brings his board to the surf's edge, hovering impossibly there a moment where the water is only inches deep.

Suddenly, he tips his shoulder and the kite—the engine of his adventure—smoothly crosses a quadrant of sky riding the same strong breeze but pulling the surfer back from the water's edge just in time, the sail on the other side of him now as he speeds away from us toward the deeper ocean.

"I can't believe it," one of us says.

Charmed sea birds appear to follow, imitating the tipping motion of the kite as it leads the otherworldly surfer toward the vanishing point on the horizon. He crashes through a wave—foam churning when the board goes under water, dragging him with it—and it looks as if the ride is over, but the surfer dependent on forces beyond his control yanks his arms back and the board passes through the breaker, hitting another, larger wave behind the first, and suddenly the surfboard is airborne, the rider lifted by his wing in a moment of transcendence as he clears the breakers and floats with abandon and pure exhilaration through air, borrowing light from the sun and, it seems, defying gravity.

~ ~ ~

It seems. No matter how beautiful, the kitesurfer does not defy gravity. He fulfills it, crashing back onto the dark water in a spray of foam as pelicans pass above.

~ ~ ~

"Owen does a spot on imitation of Yoda," Sam tells me one morning while lathering down Anna's back with sunscreen. I'm working on my arms. Later I ask Owen to perform his version of the ancient Jedi master.

The four-year-old pulls up his shoulders, lowers his chin against his chest, hunches over slightly holding his arm out as if grasping a walking stick. With his other arm he pulls together the front of the shirt as if clutching a cape.

Jokes matter.

He squints—his whole body transformed by the pose—and slowly in a boy's weird falsetto utters the mission of the enemies of the Dark Lord using the anachronistic syntax of the Jedi Master of the High Council.

"Destroy the *Sith* we must!"

Well, we all crack up.

Owen enjoys our reaction and falls out of character long enough to smile and let us know he is pleased, but, much to his mother and father's chagrin, we make him do it again and again and again.

His parents are weary of the phrase. When they play one of their family games together, it takes forever because Owen insists on being Yoda who not only talks deliberately but also makes his way across the game board at a limping pace that drives them crazy. Destroying the Sith is apparently a lifelong project.

But it is all new to the rest of us and we love it.

When we see him on the walkway to the beach or in the living room or when we're in the midst of fixing dinner, one of us will say "Destroy the Sith we must," imitating his imitation, and Owen will glower again and hunch over and say it properly, his voice rising to a creak on the name "Sith."

"Destroy the *Sith* we must!"

~ ~ ~

Destroy the Sith. We must. Unfortunately, the Sith, dedicated to the restoration of the rule of darkness to the universe, has a head start. Most of outer space is dark. Only four percent of it is visible, fiery stars and their debris, and the rest is dark matter and emptiness. What chance do Yoda and the other Jedi have?

When I was a boy I was afraid to look into the night sky through a telescope. Along the glowing edge of the moon or the rings of Saturn was all that black receding infinitely behind, hidden each clear night in plain sight. It is terrifying. First there is the cold: the scarcity of objects in motion in space results in temperatures of -455° F. Then there is the lack of light, the dark pupil of space with all but a flicker of the glowing iris gone. And then the silence: no melody, no counter-melody, no pulse. Blaise Pascal once wrote, "The eternal silence of those infinite spaces terrifies me."

A nightgown of cobwebs tossed on a skeleton. The missing hinge of the coffin. The horror of the grotto.

After The Big Bang, which in all of that silence is really The Big Light, visible matter spreads into a vast empire of black, taking myriad forms. Over time it becomes now: A curl of hair lifts slightly in the wind before falling into nonchalance around a cheek. A song, a palace of vibrating air, rises from the sound hole of a tiny instrument. Loose puzzle pieces scattered at random across a table top await a hand. Grits stirred into a big pot of boiling water slow the bubbling. An ocean wave overpowers as it yields. And a Milky Way curls through space like cream in a coffee cup.

All of today set in motion in an instant long ago and bound for no particular reason to happen.

Its uselessness a tribute to simply being.

"As we understand the world better," Sean Carroll writes, "the idea that it has a transcendent purpose seems increasingly untenable."

The spume of any day rises toward me—a rush of faces and hands and eyes and giddy cowlicks—before it suddenly recedes. And there, in that falling away, is the opposite of folly. Not wisdom, but oblivion. The Sith. Darkness. The sun tugging its unruly mane of beams into a tight ribbon before setting. The mostly empty starry sky yawning into view. Like the Alzheimer patient who glimpses in horror his demise before it fully happens, I close my eyes.

~   ~   ~

The end of mattering.

~   ~   ~

It is, as Wikipedia likes to say, time to disambiguate the word "matter." One place to start is *mater*, the word for mother in Latin. It was also the word for the heartwood at the core of a tree trunk, the source of the branch, leaf, and fruit. It is a predictable step from mother and heartwood to matter as the general word for substance, the stuff of creation.

The surprise is in the next etymological leap to matter as subject, the substance of an argument as opposed to its style of presentation, as if style were ephemeral and thoughts unadorned were lumber, solid planks of wood you could knock on with your knuckle and load into the storage bins of the mind without the embellishment of words.

After that, the meaning of the word "matter" drifts: matter as business, matter as grounds for, matter as importance—*this* is what matters—and, of course, matter as a problem: What's the matter, Maddie?

For doctors, the word means pus, the goo that suppurates from the body, the lumber of our insides gone soft.

Not surprisingly, the word takes some odd turns when it is spoken by lawyers. It stands for something requiring proof, for documents of all kinds, especially those sent in the mail bringing matter and language, separated at birth, back together again. From mother and heartwood to subpoena—we seem to have drifted far off course.

But matter is always germane, always the matter. In philosophy it means the blank, unformed, undifferentiated stuff of the universe before the creator got his hands on it. That is the way Socrates would have first understood the term as he asked questions about it with his Anaxagorean teachers in Athens. Matter as the universal ingredient. And astronomers, naming the enormous, invisible, amorphous cloud of substance that is inexorably pulling the universe apart, coined the phrase "dark matter."

Matter is the matter.

~ ~ ~

Of course, style matters too.

"*Please* don't chew with your *mouth* open!" Anna declares, her voice animated with parental anger. She is two. There is, in her voice, the weariness of an adult. She hits the first word with an emphasis created by all mothers to catch the child's attention and then drives the sentence down to the offending body part with all the verbal skill of a twenty-something parent on the verge of despair.

Brooke, the mother she is imitating, is brushing her hair and, as far as I can tell, isn't eating anything. Anna is simply aping the commands she hears spoken by her parents and teachers all day.

"She's started throwing my words back at me," Brooke says with a laugh.

"*Please* don't chew with your *mouth* open!" Anna repeats with a sly grin, and we laugh too, while she sways a bit in her pajamas, watching our reaction.

Irony, the last tone in our bag of verbal tricks. A double or nothing verbal caper. After we race through joyous, angry, shy, unhappy, sleepy, goofy, bubbly, giddy, gloomy, inquisitive, and saccharine tones of voice we discover irony, almost by mistake, the last curl in the Mobius strip of human language.

Anna looks around that curve and smiles. She is two and doesn't quite get it, but senses the power of repeating our words and tones of voice to get our attention and make us laugh.

Verbal fakery. A word folly.

"Busted, Grandpa!" Owen says when I slow down for the stop sign at a sleepy intersection but fail to come to a complete stop.

"Rolling stop," he shouts from his car seat, a phrase he's heard from some adult, and I see a Cheshire grin in the rearview mirror.

He's four. He gets it.

~ ~ ~

"Little is to be expected of that day, if it can be called a day, to which we are not awakened by our Genius," Henry David Thoreau writes in *Walden*, and he is right I know, but he wrote about a pond, not the ocean, and I have to say looking out over the wide horizon of Folly Beach, that a big, fat sunrise helps. It can wake me up. It is not just the beauty of sunrise, the "russet mantle" that Shakespeare describes, or the "quilted colors" missed by the slug-a-bed Corinna in Herrick's famous poem, "Corinna's Going A-Maying," though, goodness, that rufous glow spreading before me fills my eyes when I sit in the Crow's Nest strumming goodbye.

No, dawn on the ocean is a front seat on the universe. That is why I pull on my swim trunks and t-shirt in the semi-dark, grab the uke, and head out to this show every morning when I'm here. The geometry of its orchestrated movements grounds me, not, as the prefix "geo" suggests, on earth but among the exterior shapes and interior forms of the universe. Perhaps it releases me among them, letting me drift benignly in immensity.

I think of Caroline in footed pajamas with the sun, moon, and star designs on it, defying gravity as she strains to roll over, the movement accentuating her presence in our lives by recapitulating the motion of revolving planets. "Isn't it something," one of us says, "that we can just watch a baby!" Isn't it something, I say to myself every morning at the beach, that I can just watch the dawn! Matter is the some thing. The celestial objects are objects first and they lift me out of myself, the sun, moon, Venus, and Jupiter, dispatching ephemeral clouds, those smatterings of matter, as hardly mattering at all, clearing the way for the other less visible planets that follow prescribed paths through my sky. They frame my folly. The disks and spheres of my astronomical mobile floating in relation to each other locate me in space and time, filling my emptiness, and the warmth on my face says, against all odds, that I am at home here.

~ ~ ~

I taught the poem "L'Infinito," in one of my classes on Giacomo Leopardi—another writer I saved for my last year of college teaching. He wrote the fifteen-line masterpiece in September, 1819, at the beginning of the turbulent period of Italian reunification, and was looking for a way out of his misery that was more than just an escape.

"Always dear to me was this lonely hill," the poem begins in the Renato Poggioli translation I handed out to my students, the word "always"—"sempre"— collapsing time. A "hedge" blending in with the horizon partially "excludes the view" of the hill and the visual effect of a near feature of the landscape obscuring a distant boundary fascinated Leopardi. Any structure that "seems to stand alone above the horizon which is out of sight," he wrote in a letter about the poem, "produces a most effective and sublime contrast between the infinite and indefinite."

Leopardi called his poem an "idyll," I recall as my eye scans the shoreline at Folly Beach and pauses as usual on the house with the cupola roof that rises above a dipping horizon line half hidden by a row of bungalows. With its single lit window it stands in sharp silhouette against a sky vaguely illuminated by celestial objects at dawn. For Leopardi, the definite set beside the indefinite this way gives rise to feelings of infinity. More than that, it invites the infinite within the circle of my blurred horizon, the lit window sharing its intimate space with the sun and Venus and the stars beyond. Infinity does not frighten Leopardi as it does me. Instead he is overwhelmed and comforted at once. He has a lesson to teach me. In the presence of such immensity "my thought is drowned," he wrote in the last lines of the poem, and, as if speaking to me, adds "foundering is sweet to me in this sea."

~ ~ ~

Everyone else has gone to bed, and I am alone in the Dinosaur Room, the name that the kids gave to the children's playroom, staring at a loose piece of the half-finished Ludicrous Library and remembering Zeno's famous puzzle.

Zeno argued that each of us is frozen on points that keep us forever apart. He lived in Elea, a Greek city marked by treachery, intrigue, and distrust which may have contributed to his world view. He proved his lonely proposition with a clever paradox: Achilles chases down a slower runner who has a head start, but never reaches him because to do so he must first arrive at the spot where the slower runner has already been. He can never achieve his goal because he is forever halfway to halfway to halfway there, falling behind in an infinite regression of bisections.

We live on scattered puzzle pieces floating further away from each other like the stars in the universe, I think. No wonder…

Abruptly I stop, angry with myself.

"The downstairs doorway," I mutter, awash in the sounds of the ocean.

That's right. I forgot to take Owen to see the downstairs doorway. Maybe we can get down there tomorrow. Or maybe Zeno's right and we'll never get more than halfway to halfway there. I pause at the stairwell heading toward the doorway that fascinates my grandson, peering over the wooden guardrail. The hallway is dark, but there must be a moonlit shimmer coming in at the sill because I can make out a wooden cabinet with carefully arranged clutter on it: a large, round thermometer, an oriental fan, old bricks, and various decorative paddle boards with a rattan wall hanging flanked by several watercolor prints on the wall above it. The doorway itself is partially hidden from view, but the glow animates the scene. This is the place of secrets and whispers. The forbidden. The shimmer you know is just around the corner. Shafts of sunlight fading in the woods. No wonder Owen wants to see it. The place of time elastic. Now and never.

Four

THIS SUNRISE IS like yesterday's except that there are two of them, one happening above the clouds in spreading glory while I strum the ukulele and the other below in a glimmering puddle on the ocean.

I'm playing "Planxty Eleanor Plunkett," a stately tune composed for harp by the blind Irish minstrel Turlough O'Carolan and never, as far as I know, played on the ukulele. The origins of the Gaelic word "Planxty" are unclear, but it has come to mean "in praise of" or "to the glory of" and is sung as a tribute to a person.

While I strum, my eyes follow the twin sunrises, one growing like a blaze in the forge of morning and the other darkening and smoldering in embers. It is cell division. Birth. A supernova of dwarf twins.

"To the glory of"—yes.

The song suits the sky.

Blind O'Carolan could not have seen this, I realize, looking out on the double glow and following the tune up to a ringing "a" at the twelfth fret, but he would have felt the glow of such a beginning as warmth on his face.

I would hope so, I think, as the day rises to his melody.

Days measure lives, the new day emerging out of the death of the old. What if we had no days? What if we knew just "day" or just "night?" No doubling. Just one long O'Carolan night. A mono-nocturne.

I like a marker. A herald. It is the "each" part of Annie Dillard's "each day is a god" that lends divinity to the morning. It is the plural "days" in Emerson's line "no one suspects the days to be gods" that fills the sky with this unearthly light.

Division makes doubling possible.

The gold dome of the brighter sun breaks above the clouds during my second time through the melody, contracting the beams into itself—a focused glare that suffuses the rest of the light turning the sky above into the pale blue of morning, while the darker sun, buried in the ocean, becomes the night left behind. I watch a couple emerge out of the blue and gold holding hands and walking toward me at the end of a glowing pathway leading to morning, some Adam and Eve of the new day, and bring the song with its slow and stately minor setting to an end on a major chord.

A day like no other arrives.

~ ~ ~

By the time Owen joins me in the Crow's Nest, I have gone through my celestial repertoire: "Here Comes the Sun," "Carolina Moon," and "You Are My

Sunshine." The sun is well up when he penguin-wobbles toward me wearing a swimsuit, t-shirt, and sunlight on his cheek. I'm down to the cornier tunes. My shtick. Of course I drag out, "Ukulele Lady" and he gets a kick out of the part about the lady who sings "when it's cool and shady" and "where the tricky wicky wackies woo." Well, who doesn't? I sing "Ain't She Sweet" and "Five Foot Two" followed by the Sasquatch version which put my sweet "gal" at "Eight Foot Two."

Owen watches as I sing, and I watch back. He smiles broadly, but the sunlight coming from over his right shoulder is just enough to make him squint a bit, the side of his eyes turning down slightly to complement the smile. His hair is uncombed, but it is a thick, dark brown that falls naturally in place around the cowlick at the hair line. Sunlight plays along his creamy smooth skin.

No, play is the wrong word. Sunlight doesn't play, at least not here at the beach. It is an unrelenting glow, accentuating the curves that Owen's skin offers freely, carving dimples under his eyes, and flowing down where the skin dips along the curve at his chin. Sunlight has nothing to offer. It plunders beauty that is already there. "Here comes the sun," I sing, acknowledging sunlight's long journey through space, but it arrives on our shores empty handed to lift us out of darkness for its pleasure.

In celebration, I pull out all of the stops with a new song: "Iko Iko," the hit recorded by the Dixie Cups in 1965 that comes from the traditional call and response challenges of two battling tribes at a Mardi Gras parade.

"My grandma and your grandma," it begins, "sittin' by the fire." A song made of taunts. In it two grandmothers from different tribes face off, followed by men from the tribes dressed in red and green. The chorus, a string of words from many languages, includes the refrain: "Jock-a-mo fin-a-ney."

No one knows what the phrase means. It's a jumble. A word folly. There are as many guesses as there are versions of it. James "Sugar Boy" Crawford, who recorded the original version, explained in an interview with *Offbeat.com* that Jock-a-mo means "brother John," or "jokester," or "Giacomo;" Jock-a-mo fin a ney means "kiss my ass," or "John is dead"; Iko means "I go," or "pay attention," or "gold," or "hiking around," the words coming from French, Yoruba, or Italian. And "Jock" could be "Chock" which changes everything!

If I had to select from that list of meanings for the word "Iko," I would choose "pay attention." John is a brother, a jokester, and probably dead, but he can kiss my ass. I'll pay attention to this day that no king can give me. It is mine for the watching. So "chock *you*." That's my translation, and I chant it loudly now and play a syncopated rhythm on the ukulele causing Owen to rock back and forth in front of me, the sunlight on his cheek following his penguin sway. Now we're swaying together. When I get to the chorus he mouths the words with me and we are both smiling now.

The song ends abruptly when I slap my palm over the strings causing Owen to laugh.

"Grandpa," he says, "you sing the best songs."

~ ~ ~

55

Maddie spends most of her time at the beach jumping waves. She is too young to go out alone, so we take turns with her, standing in the ocean, holding hands, waiting for the waves to gather and slam into her. Last year we went with her in pairs and there is an iconic family photo of Folly Beach from that time with Sam and Nessa on either side lifting her by her tiny arms as a wave splashes against her. But now she is old enough to go with us one at a time. Sometimes she turns her back on the waves, letting the white water break over her shoulders as she screams. Other times she takes them head on, her face getting the brunt of the exploding surf, and she quickly wipes the water out of her eyes and prepares for the next blast.

Anna likes the water this year too. She charges down to the edge swinging her arms while some parent tries to catch up to her, her body language saying "Anna do it!" as she hits the surf's edge. When she is knee deep she stops as the waves dissipate and spread on the shore. White water foams around her thighs and she laughs out loud and runs back to the sand, ready to try again.

Owen does not go far into the water yet. He hangs back at the surf's edge. Sometimes he sits in the water looking a little unhappy, watching Maddie jumping waves, as if he is waiting for her to grow bored with her game and come back to the sand to play. But as long as there are waves, Maddie does not tire of leaping them.

~ ~ ~

Owen is not the only Harvey grandchild with an
individual walk. Maddie is the most determined little
ambulator. Even when she is not angry, she stomps off.
She is not always trying to get somewhere, but she acts
as if she is. When she talks her eyes go wide and she
waves her hands in the air just like her mother, and her
manner of walking is a version of that. She walks as if
she is jumping waves, chest out, face set for the blast,
arms in fists at her side. Sometimes she and Owen like
to run together through the Crow's Nest on the
boardwalk toward the beach, he wearing a goofy smile
and pumping his arms, she with mouth wide open
waving her arms wildly toward the sea.

Anna sashays like her mother with a slightly
exaggerated sway of her hips. A serious little girl, she
often purses her lips as she walks, as if she has
something on her mind and when she gets to you she
might, if you are lucky, whisper it in your ear. She might
not. I always get the sense that she is talking in her head
while she is walking toward me, rehearsing what she
intends to say, which gives her little promenade a
meditative air. She rarely hurries and prefers to arrive
stylishly, rather than early, often sweeping her hair back
from her eyes when she finally reaches her destination
and squinting while she waits for you to lean forward.
This year she has taken to running toward the water,
mincing up to it in tiny steps and stopping when the
waves lap over her toes. She bends forward and laughs
or says something that only the ocean can hear.

Caroline is too young to have a walk, but I can
picture it now. She stands—a mighty, wobbling

building of a baby girl—and staggers a bit, each foot
coming down right where it started and then with a
laugh lunges forward in a stampede of ever quickening
baby steps before tumbling face down.

~ ~ ~

The Dixie Cups learned "Iko Iko" when they were
girls attending Mardi Gras parades. It grew out of the
chants as one black neighborhood group, disguised in
the colors of its "tribe," challenged another. The
recording was apparently a spontaneous event, the
Dixie Cups accompanying themselves with what they
could find in the studio, tapping an ashtray, a coke
bottle, and a drum playing two separate rhythms
simultaneously. The Dixie Cups keep the syncopation
going for the entire song, creating a cross rhythm, that
fools the ear.

The listener cannot tell which rhythm is really
driving the tune.

I can't play polyrhythms on the ukulele, but I can
imitate the sound by creating a simple rhythm with my
fingers and playing an off-rhythm beat with my thumb.
It is like syncopation, but playing the main rhythm and
off-beat with equal emphasis makes it hard to tell which
is the prevailing beat. The rhythms swell. The sound
surrounds me. It is the rhythm of creation. I hear it in
ocean and undertow, breath and heartbeat, the clatter
of separate households waking.

Am I waving goodbye or hello?

C. K. Ladzekpo, the San Francisco Bay Area
composer and choreographer, says I'm doing both at

once. He writes on his website called "The Myth of Cross Rhythms" that "cross-beats can symbolize the challenging moments or emotional stress we all encounter." For him cross rhythm, in which the main beat is lost among secondary ones, fortifies us for those times when our main goals are regularly thwarted. "Playing crossbeats while fully grounded in the main beats, prepares one for maintaining a life-purpose while dealing with life's challenges." He points out that many languages in sub-Saharan Africa have no word for rhythm: "From the African viewpoint, the rhythms represent the very fabric of life itself" symbolizing "interdependence in human relationships." When Maddie hears me play my faux cross rhythms, her shoulders move back and forth instinctively and the hem of her gown sways in a separate direction. Soon she can't stand the ambiguity of the extra beat slipped into my aloha and has to run off.

~ ~ ~

"George Gershwin wrote 'Summertime' at Folly Beach," I say. We are on the porch finishing up lunch in the hot hours of the day. I lean back in the deck chair and survey the waves: a strip of white water that forms at the far end of the beach slowly churns my way dissipating in its undertow, followed by another strip of white, and another, and another.

Matt is bent over his iPhone, his fingers glowing. "It says here it's a myth."

I take a sip of my drink and squint at the water and sky. "Then it's a nice myth," I say. A silence falls over the group, and I keep watching the sea, the rhythm of crashing followed by withdrawal.

Later I read in Stratton Lawrence's book that Gershwin did write "Summertime" and the other songs from *Porgy and Bess* while at Folly Beach, but it was in the winter of 1934, not the summer.

The idea that Gershwin was inspired by the beach probably is a myth. He experimented with polyrhythms and other African musical techniques while composing the music for his opera and visited black churches in the Charleston area absorbing the cadences of their music. That was his inspiration.

The waves were a distraction.

"This place is different from any place I've seen or lived in before," Gershwin wrote about Folly Beach. "It's been hard for me to work here, as the wild waves, playing the role of siren, beckon me every time I get stuck, which is often." The secondary beat of the waves on the beach lured him away from the main beat during the winter of his summertime, "causing many hours to be knocked into a thousand useless bits."

~ ~ ~

Night terrors, or *pavor nocturnus* is a sleep disorder that looks like a waking nightmare, when being asleep and being awake look alike. It usually happens in the first few hours of sleep, roaring alive in a child during "the deepest stage of non-rapid eye movement sleep," the Mayo clinic website explains. It is sometimes called "slow-wave sleep."

"In this state," Nessa explains when she talks about Maddie's sleep terrors, she is "inconsolable." She may seem to be awake, her eyes looking about, but her face wears the expression of panic as if she is running away from great danger. She doesn't remember the dreams the next day, but we see the terror on her face as she runs through the cartoon walls of *pavor nocturnus* leaving behind a row of silhouettes.

"Slow wave sleep." The muffled tranquility under the breakers. The calm of the womb. No wonder Maddie immerses herself obsessively in the ocean waves just beyond the reach of her terror.

~ ~ ~

"Too much information," I realize, closing the website on "Night Terror." What am I to make of it all? When asked about the duty of the writer to inform the reader, the author Maggie Nelson leans into her microphone and says "those who come from a literary end believe the mission to inform is a lost cause."

So I rummage the beach for metaphors.

~ ~ ~

The Civil War started "within earshot" of Folly Beach. Before dawn on April 12, 1861, Confederates stationed on James Island lobbed a mortar shell that exploded over Fort Sumpter. Soon after the fall of the fort, Union troops created a foothold in the area by driving Confederate troops from Folly Beach. They built the first roads on the island under the protection of a canopy of thick foliage and dug in at the beachhead for the remainder of the war. They used the island to bombard Charleston with a battery of Parrott cannons and as a staging area for attacks on James and Morris islands.

Life on Folly Beach during the war was grim. Garbage piled up in the summer heat attracting rats and fleas. "Water quality was poor," writes Lawrence, and "soldiers subsisted on meagre food rations and the occasional bottle of scotch smuggled into camp." Most of the casualties were from malnutrition, dehydration, disease, and dysentery. In the summer, tents along the edge of the woods faced on the ocean to catch sea breezes, but for much of the time soldiers huddled in "splinterproofs," low bunkers made of barrels, rocks, wood, and sand designed to protect them from bombardment. The only battle on the island happened on May 10, 1862 when 120 Confederate troops attacked in an attempt to test Yankee troop strength, but Union troops huddled in their splinterproofs in order to conceal their numbers, and did not return fire.

I want to call the splinterproofs follies due to their haphazard construction made with things at hand, but when I see a line drawing of one in *The Pictorial Field Book of the Civil War* by Benson John Lossing I realize that splinterproofs were elaborately constructed dugouts made out of neatly stacked barrels and boards, propped against vegetation, such as a Carolina palmetto, for support and camouflaged with sand and broken shells. I think of a Union soldier huddled in one as bombs explode overhead. War and folly don't mix, and all the folly has been drained away from these thoroughly utilitarian bunkers, grottoes where men curl up and merely survived a rain of bullets and shrapnel.

~ ~ ~

A grotto is the opposite of a folly. It is shadow, silhouette, and grave. A downstairs doorway to a place with a secret. Barbara Jones defines a grotto as a "rocky cave that may be natural, or nature improved, or entirely artificial, being made of rocks, and sometimes decorated with shells." She calls them "pleasant" but is quick to add that our word "grotesque" is derived from "grotto" and that the word has over time acquired a meaning gloomier than "noble rocks and pretty shells."

Naomi Miller in *Heavenly Caves: Reflections on a Garden Grotto* agrees, pointing out that the Italian word "grottesche" was used for the hidden "mural decorations and capricious ornament" discovered during the excavation of Nero's underground vaults. Caves, she explains, are associated with the celebration of mysteries beyond human understanding: "with rites of birth and death, magic ceremonies, mantic powers," and "erotic bacchanalian orgies." In *The Aeneid* a grotto is the "haunt of Nymphs" who live under "the brow" of a rocky outcropping and sit on seats carved "in living stone." Grottoes were often used as the labs for experiments in alchemy, too, and for Horace the grotesqueries of the cave were the source of fantasy and make believe.

This is where Maddie screams in night terror.

~ ~ ~

While I fix a drink for Nessa and me, Matt gets to work on a math problem I gave him. How many combinations of notes can I make on a ukulele? Assuming my fingers can stretch to all of the notes on the seven-inch keyboard—which they nearly can do—how many choices do I have when I make a chord?

Maddie is asleep at last. Like her mom and grandfather, she has trouble settling down at bedtime, and Nessa had to go into her room to read books and talk and sing to her for more than an hour. But she's down for the night now. And Nessa flops into one of the porch chairs, her fingers cupped in the shape of a cocktail glass. That's my cue.

It's dark now and the ocean is only a sound to us. Is it a cradle endlessly rocking as Whitman would have us to believe? A lullaby to lull us? Dave Gallo, the director of special projects at Woods Hole, has a different metaphor. "I think it works like a symphony," he said on NPR's *Here and Now*.

Tonight I hope Whitman's right. We could all use some sleep.

When I get back from the kitchen with a drink for Nessa's claw and one for me, Matt has just finished working in the dark on his cell phone, his face lit. He's ready to explain the problem.

"You say there are twelve frets on the ukulele and there is also the open string. This means each of the four strings is capable of thirteen notes. So"—he tilts the screen of his cell phone my way to show me the problem—"you multiply thirteen times thirteen four times: 13 x 13 x 13 x 13."

64

He taps enter and the answer appears in glowing letters: 28,561.

Later, as I try to nod off in bed I remember Matt's number and think about playing in the Crow's Nest the next morning. When I choose a chord it will be one out of 28,561 possible combinations. It seems like a lot, but it is just the beginning of my choices, because when I hit the next chord it compounds the possibilities making it 28,561 combinations to the second power. And the next chord and the next. And then there are single notes and paired notes and those nice three-string chords I like to run up the neck compounding the possibilities exponentially. Over a lifetime of full, four-string chords, and single notes, and paired strings, and triple strings I make a symphony.

Not a lullaby, I think with a sigh, slow to fall asleep.

~ ~ ~

Clocks measure rhythms, not time. They swing, as Gershwin might say. The earth swings around the sun measuring a year. The moon swings around the earth measuring a month. The earth swings around its axis against a backdrop of stars measuring a day. The swinging pendulum in a grandfather clock measures out the minutes. The balance wheel in a wrist watch swings out the seconds.

Time itself goes on untouched.

So when scientists "saw a need for much more precise measurement," writes James Jespersen and Jane Fitz-Randolph in *From Sundials to Atomic Clocks*, they "began looking at other things that swing." An electrical current alternates at 60 hertz per second and the tuning fork in an electric wrist watch is set to vibrate at 360 cycles per second, dividing time into thinner slices. Quartz crystals when activated by an electrical current divide time into *mega*hertz with millions of swings per second.

"What swings faster?" the writers ask.

Atoms do.

An atom of cesium, used in the clocks that helped confirm the theories of Albert Einstein, emit microwave signals at a rate of 9,192,631,770 times per second.

But there is a limit. Atoms with higher frequencies emit uncertain amounts of energy. When measuring the swings, the "more we want to know about *what* happened, the less we can know *when* it happened, and vice versa."

It is the uncertainty principle which Jespersen and Fitz-Randolph admit "seems to be a fundamental feature of nature."

The polyrhythm at the beating heart of things.

"From the African viewpoint," writes C. K. Ladzekpo, "the very fabric of life itself."

~ ~ ~

Owen is not alone in elastic time. Bashō lives there too and invites the rest of us in. He was the first writer to clip the short *hokku* opening from the longer *renga*, a collaborative poem that young people in Japan used to entertain each other at parties, and turn it into a tiny time machine known as *haiku*. On his journey to the interior, Bashō and a fellow traveler crossed the Natorigawa River in early spring to visit at sunset the Shrine of Tenjin, the god of letters. They were led by a painter named Kaemon who often guided writers to sites made famous by poets, and as farewell gifts he gave each of the travelers a pair of straw sandals with blue straps. Bashō gave Kaemon a haiku in return:

> To have blue irises
> blooming on one's feet—
> walking sandal straps.

I lie on the beach with my cap pulled over my eyes and smile as the image forms in my mind. The gift blooms as brightly as it did for Bashō in the spring of 1689.

~ ~ ~

In a way, everything happens all the time. The downstairs doorway opens on yesterday, today, and tomorrow.

My friend, the writer Jill Christman, teaches that an author should anchor personal nonfiction in a certain time in the narrator's life. Grounded in a particular now, the story gains focus, because the reader knows everything before this now is in the past and everything after it has not yet happened even though, in the author's life, it has. Ignoring this simple time marker unmoors the reader and is a typical beginner's mistake.

Unfortunately that is not where I live anymore. For me events swing in a perpetual subjunctive mood where the future is already over and done with, the ephemeral present barely exists at all, and the past fills with hope and never goes away. Where the closest thing to a time marker is the word "if."

Lost is where I am most alive.

The fort that shimmers in my mind when I conceive it and tomorrow when I remember it and today when I write it is the same fort. It is what the fort means. My Platonic fort. What other fort do I have?

The rest is sand.

Is it even possible to get ahead of myself in such a book?

But I am. I haven't even thought up the sand fort yet—though it's only a matter of time.

~ ~ ~

Barbara came up with the idea of bringing Ladderball, a game she saw last year on her walks along the beach. It consists of two plastic, ladder-shaped targets separated by about twenty paces in the sand. Each player has three sets of paired, heavy plastic balls tethered together like bolas. The goal is to toss the bola so that it wraps around the rungs of the ladder. Different points are given out for each rung hit, with the lowest rung worth the most, and the player who reaches twenty-one points wins.

With the help of Owen and Maddie, Matt and Nessa put together the Ladderball game which required joining a series of plastic tubes to make the three-tiered "ladder." Nessa read the directions while Matt laid out the pieces according to size. When they were done and the two ladders stood intact beside their empty boxes, we marched them down to the beach, Matt carrying one and I the other, and staked them to the sand for a game.

Ladderball, we soon discovered, is harder than it looks. My first bola overshot the target entirely, the balls flailing in the air like a wounded bird before crashing in sand way beyond its goal. Matt got the hang of it pretty quickly, tossing the ball with a gentle wrist action and an upward release of the hand that caused the bola to float fully extended toward the target like a rotating wheel, hitting the rung, and twisting around the bar with a snap. Once in a while a bola would hit the ladder in such a way that it would climb down the rungs, like a gymnast on uneven bars, landing for top points on the bottom rung.

Despite its floppy flight there is a goofy grace about the Ladderball bola, the way it hangs with two balls balanced on a string midflight, defies gravity with a desperate waving of arms, and, employing weight, inertia and centrifugal motion, latches on like an acrobat, one end of the bola wound around the bar while the ball at the other end swings in a pendulum motion, scoring by marking time.

~ ~ ~

Most of the time—when you are not Owen and not reading this book—time goes in one direction. Arthur Stanley Eddington called this the "arrow of time" in *The Nature of the Physical World* published in 1928. Since entropy, increasing randomness, is "the only thing which cannot be undone" in the universe, the arrow of time always points one way, toward the future. Time is not the pendulum motion of the Ladderball bola. Time *is* the Ladderball bola, an increasingly battered toy hurtling through an increasingly random universe like some wounded bird.

"Destroy the Sith, we must!" says Owen in his Yoda pose, deflecting the arrow with his mind.

~ ~ ~

While the others are jumping waves with Maddie or chasing Anna as she charges the water or playing Ladderball with Owen, I'm babysitting Caroline again while she sits propped up in her tent. Wearing my ball cap and a blue t-shirt I lean into the cool shadows of her hideaway and sing her a song about the moon shining over Carolina. Several days ago she cried, but today she is calm and wide eyed. The good news: she can't even crawl away, though she seems to pay more attention to her toes than to me.

I like a captive audience.

Last year Anna was my audience. While she sat on her blanket in the shadows of the beach umbrella wearing her pink sun dress and matching sneakers and poking at the sand with a yellow plastic shovel, I sang her song, "You Are My Sunshine," on my blue ukulele. She couldn't get away either. Older last year than Caroline now, she sat up just fine but she was still only a year old and hadn't learned to stand or walk. So while I sang to her, my face partially hidden under a straw hat, she squinted and gave me a puzzled look.

Singing to Caroline as if she were Anna deflects the arrow, the future becoming the past merely by writing "as if."

But this arrow-of-time business is tricky. This year, on one of our first afternoons at the beach house, Anna, who is no longer the baby I sang to in the tent, is able to walk up to me while I am playing ukulele in The Crow's Nest. She and her daddy had been practicing. So when I sing "You Are My Sunshine," she joins right in, singing the words. She sways back and forth in a flower print dress that belonged to Maddie last year, and while I sing she steps closer, the arrow righted and pointed ahead once again, her eyes going back and forth between my face and the ukulele. Her voice is a little shy, but she nails the words and when it is over she runs back to her dad, puts her head in his lap, and glances back at me smiling.

The arrow runs right through me.

~   ~   ~

Like the mind of the writer the pelicans hover— patiently, dreamily—before they drop for the kill.

~   ~   ~

I pluck my ukulele and feel the string snap off of my fingertip. I strum a chord and feel the vibrations through my t-shirt in my chest and gut. Does the matter of song matter? The snap and the tingling in my chest say yes. The sound may be amplified by an empty box of exotic wood and emerge from the emptiness of a sound hole—an echoing that can turn an eye and

71

enthrall listeners—but the box and the hole are not empty at all. They form a chamber stuffed with billowing veils of vibrating air setting in motion William Butler Yeats' famous dancer, the one he can't tell from the dance, in my case a figure wearing a hula skirt and a lily behind her right ear, floating in a swirl of scarves from a blackened sound hole under my fingertips, and swaying on the dashboard of my song.

Matter and mattering are not so easily disentwined.

~ ~ ~

At night I walk out to the Crow's Nest with drink in hand, lean back against the railing, and look out into the night of strewn stars and a crescent moon. Waves glimmer like sequins against the thick velour of the ocean. All of the colors of the day have receded leaving this evening dress. Only the roar of the daytime remains, the main rhythm crashing in, inchoate and throbbing, the counter-rhythm of withdrawal whispering something I can't quite make out.

Matt joins me.

"Hi Dad."

He leans back against the opposite railing taking in the scene. My quiet child, the mathematician.

Eventually we find ourselves talking about the shape and size of the universe that we are watching. I tell him that I have been reading about the multiverse, the idea that vastly different universes can exist simultaneously. Despite the mathematical precision used to conjure up these various universes they remain pretty vague, but if these scientists are right, the panorama stretching from horizon to horizon that Matt and I are looking into is the inner edge of a drop in an ocean of possible universes.

"Here is where physics and mathematics merge," Matt says. He has heard all of this before. "Physicists can posit other universes with different rules than our own and mathematicians can insist that they be internally coherent." He looks back at me, crosses his arms, and laughs.

"But we have no idea if any of these universes exist."

Silent again, we look up into the black and glittering scene where celestial dancers sweep onto the floor giddy with evening and a dress hem disappears behind a bedroom door.

~ ~ ~

Decorating the dark is a labor of love. Follies which bedeck the sky can be built quickly but grottoes, like the many that were created in England during the Enlightenment, take decades to dig and a lifetime or two to beautify with seashells.

Shell reflection can be wavering and autumnal, like the glow in the grotto at Merewood with its darkened shell room containing two large cranes holding "swags of shell flowers in their shell beaks" caught, Barbara Jones writes, like a "fly in amber" under a light that "thickens to a golden haze." Or it can be brilliant like the Lion's Den grotto of Thomas Golden in Bristol which overpowers its stunning shell decorations with water works supplied at one time by a fire engine.

In grottoes, whelks and conchs with seductive wave-lips call from below. Glitter on top of glitter from the Age of Light illuminates the path down, transforming the blackness in the way that stars fleeing from each other into the absolute dark of space fill the vault of the night sky. Matt and I lean against railings in the Crow's Nest and silently gaze at constellations above, but, of course, in space there is no above or below, no up or down.

Grottoes are the celestial night sky dragged underground.

~ ~ ~

The opposite of folly is the silence of empty space.

~ ~ ~

"Grandpa," Owen asks, "what do you write in that little book?"

He is talking about the composition book that I keep in my shirt pocket, a smaller version of the kind I used to write in in school. This one has a blue mottled cover, eighty lined pages, and measures 4½ by 3¼ inches. I have reinforced the top and bottom of the cover with scotch tape to protect it from wear and have written my name, the date 6/17/14 when I began the book, and the name Folly Beach in the space for the title.

"I want that book grandpa," Owen insists with a mock seriousness holding out one hand. One eyebrow turns down to indicate that he's all business, but there is a little twitch of a smile at the corner of his frown.

When I give him the book he flips through the pages like an inspector searching for evidence, nodding approvingly as if he could read.

"Lots of tangled up lines," he says, summing up my career.

He does what he does with all books, checking it for bookmarks which he keeps before discarding the book over his shoulder. As he runs off to pull more books out of the shelves with his cousin, I pick up my notebook and open it to a blank page.

"Grandpa," I write, "what do you write in that little book?"

~ ~ ~

What *do* I write in my little book?

The impossible I guess. Life as it is happening. It is a little inconvenient, having to pull the book out on the beach or while having a cocktail to jot down a thought or a remark, but my family is used to it. I want the words before they disappear, the first wave of life's polyrhythm.

The note on the vibrating string before the palm silences it.

The sunrise before the crow cuts a hole in the sky.

Event before insight.

A bookmark lodged in the now.

Lots of tangled up lines.

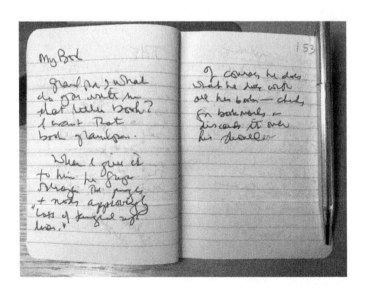

Five

THE WINDOW IN THE HOUSE with the cupola roof is lit yellow again, but the rest of the dawn sky is black. As my eyes grow accustomed to the dark I see why. A large bank of clouds rising above the horizon has swallowed up the sun allowing nighttime to linger.

Dark dawn.

Down, down-up down, down-up down I strum, hitting the opening chords of my Beatle song in my attempt to conjure up the sun, and the sky begins to lighten to a pearly color as clouds and houses and shoreline emerge.

Suddenly, a fold in the fabric of the sky glows and like a word rising to awareness without effort or strain the sun parts the curtain of clouds, illuminating the scene. A beachcomber carrying a stick heads away from me at the water's edge, a small dog padding beside him, both in silhouette heading toward the light, and a path of gold spreads across the waves.

Barbara calls these rays of sunlight descending from a bank of clouds "And the Lord says" and today they do seem to be heralds of the big event as the sun itself catches up with its beams, shoulders aside the gloom, and smiles down on us.

~ ~ ~

The crow is not just a symbol. When it lights this close on the PVC pipe and shakes its wings at me, it is an animal. A claw, secured from behind by a back talon, grips the plastic firmly, sable wings fold along the flank in primary, secondary, and tertial layers, and the crown, a flat silhouette from some angles, has a shape rounded by morning glow.

Matter matters.

Hey, crow, I think, setting down my ukulele to watch.

The black bird clacks, shifting positions on the pipe, and surveys the scene, the ultimate Lord of the Crow's Nest. Uneasy in my presence, it struts, flicking its tail, sometimes facing me and other times turning its back. It stops, lowers its head beneath the level of the PVC pipe and tilts the bead of one eye my way for a closer look, but something below catches its attention, and it leans into the morning air, releases its talons, spreads its wings, and swoops down on a crushed hamburger bun along the fence line. One of the kids probably dropped it yesterday from the porch above. The hunk is too heavy to lift, so the crow tears at it with claws and beak, mandibles ripping away the crust, when two mockingbirds attack from above, landing on either side of the wad of bread, their wings spread in an aggressive display. After a brief scuffle, the crow retreats, a shred of the bun in its beak, first to our porch rail and then, seeing me, to the railing of the porch two houses down, its muscular shoulders and broad wings gleaming in sunlight as it descends.

~ ~ ~

Commotion in the kitchen. Maddie, Owen, and Anna are there sitting up to the counter on their stools. Nessa sets out vanilla, sugar, milk and three eggs for French toast. Matt, with hair still tousled from sleep, sneaks behind the hubbub to get a cup of coffee trying to look inconspicuous. He knows what French toast means with this crowd. Sam mans the oven. The kids have been awake for an hour or so and already had breakfast, but as Nessa lifts three eggs carefully from the carton and sets them in the bowl, they take notice. Owen lifts one egg and says he wants to help, and Nessa says yes, as she eases the egg out of Owen's fist, moving instinctively through the giddiness all around her. She's done this before.

"Of course you can help!"

Nessa has a naturally joyful personality. She laughs easily and does not take herself too seriously. The word that comes to mind when I think of her is 'sunny' or maybe 'bubbly'. But this morning she is tired. Maddie did not sleep well last night and all of our morning talk and laughter kept Nessa from falling back to sleep after Maddie got up. While pulling the carton of milk out of the refrigerator, she lays her head on my chest and sighs, and when Owen lifts the egg a little too high to crack it on the edge of the bowl, I see her purse her lips and close her eyes, fighting back against weariness.

When Owen drops the whole egg in the bowl, weariness turns to surprise,

"Oh my goodness!" she says, laughing, as she fishes the shell daintily out of the bowl with her fingers. Owen the little performer lifts both hands in the air and looks around the room to see who noticed, but Nessa doesn't miss a beat.

"It's your turn, Maddie," she announces, setting the broken shell in a saucer beside her with dripping fingers and sliding the bowl to her daughter with her elbow.

~ ~ ~

Brooke lowers the strap of Anna's swimsuit, a red-striped one-piece trimmed with bands of pink polka dots, one strap decorated with a pink rosette. Her skin under the suit is pearly and gleaming, and as Brooke rubs in the sunscreen Anna loses balance and wobbles a bit, so her mother grabs her arm to steady her while still rubbing.

The act of rubbing in sunscreen is a holding on, a claiming, but what we hold onto is slippery and loose in our grip.

I rub my arms while Barbara does my back and then we switch.

The folds of her skin give way to fingertips, resisting the circular pattern of my fingers as they embrace it, the oils smoothing out the motion. Flesh is tawny—a supple protection—vulnerable to scrapes and burns, but tough to touch and accepting of this buttery attention. Children don't want what the skin wants, it seems. Nessa works on Maddie who squirms and turns her face away. She crosses her arms, but her mother, unperturbed, keeps working the oil into her arms and chest and cheeks.

Matt steps into the mix, shaking a yellow tube of sunscreen, his eye on Owen.

Intimacy. Exposure. Touch.

All of us in various states of undress in the room together, clinging to slippery bodies we have but cannot keep.

This rubbing is generative. I rub a leg that has fallen asleep to bring it back to life. A lover rubs a shoulder. A woman rubs her stomach between contractions.

Skin brings us together.

Why do we put up with our bodies? John Donne asks in his poem "The Ecstasy." My students looked up when I rephrased the question for them, but I directed their attention back to the page in their books. The answer is in the poem, I tell them. "Look there!"

Bodies holding hands in the churn of ocean waves.

Bodies in a swirl of sheets.

Full of longing.

Letting go before holding on before letting go.

"We owe them thanks," the poet writes, "because they thus, / Did us to us first convey."

~ ~ ~

I wake up from under my ball cap, and all I can see is the concentric circular stitching of the underside of the bill shading out the sun, but I can feel the radiance of the beach all around me. I must have taken a nap. I lift one corner of the bill to see a Ford pickup marked

Fire and Rescue in bold red and gold lettering beyond me on the sand backing up to the water with a catamaran in tow. What are *they* doing here? I push back my cap and lift up on one elbow to take in the scene. No sign of a rescue in progress. Barbara is reading beside me. Matt and Angie are with the kids down at the water doing fine. Bathers walk up and down the beach casually. And the crew of the boat wearing bathing suits, t-shirts, and flip flops do not look like they are on duty.

Still the men swarm around the catamaran like commandoes. They remove the wheel base of the platform and drop duffle bags of gear from the truck which they unload, checking the items as they lift them from the bag. Two of the men don vests and raise the masthead, mainsail, and jib but there is something wrong so they lower the jib and try again. Methodical. Careful. This looks like work, I think as I fall back into my chair, but, when the sail is fully erect, the silky cloth with yellow, red, and maroon stripes above the numbers 64691 swells effortlessly and forms a graceful arc against blue sky.

The two crew members stand at the bow of the double hulled craft and pull it into the surf. Quickly they slide to the side, let the sail pull the craft deeper into the waves, and leap aboard.

"They're off," I say, while taking pictures on my phone.

"That was easy," Barbara says sarcastically as she surveys the team, leaning forward to get a better look.

I remember my first dawn at the beach, the incandescent cirrus clouds tilted toward the sun like a fleet of catamarans on their way to a regatta dragging an ocean of beauty behind. This sail against sky, I wonder—this petal of light that the crew struggled to raise—is it work or folly? Is it a byproduct of their labor and method and care, the mere side-effect of discipline and energy? Or is beauty their secret mission?

The sail tips precariously this way and that as the men settle in and we watch the boat head straight out to the horizon and disappear leaving the wheelbase and a pair of flip-flops behind in the sand.

~ ~ ~

In April of 1879 in the town of Hauterives the French postman Ferdinand Cheval tripped on a stone and became inspired to create one of the world's great follies, the Palais Idéal. "I was walking very fast," he explains in a passage from the Wikipedia article on him, "when my foot caught on something that sent me stumbling a few meters away." Fifteen years earlier, Cheval had a dream of "a palace, castle, or caves" which embarrassed him because of its oddity. Fearing ridicule, he told no one about it. But years later when he had "almost forgotten" his dream and "wasn't thinking of it at all," he literally stumbled onto a way to bring his dream to life.

The stone was a "strange shape" of three dark, raised layers of sandstone looking a bit like a stack of irregularly formed pancakes. "It's a sandstone shaped by water and hardened by the power of time," as

Cheval described it, though "molded" might almost be a better word since the shapes appear animated and have a kind of intentionality to them as if they are flowing deliberately in several directions at once.

Cheval began his folly by laying this stone in front of a cave near a small pool that he called "The Source of Life." "À la source de la vie j'ai puisé mon génie," he writes in the French Wikipedia article on his life. "At the source of life I found my genius," I read in the English version. He spent thirty-three years on his masterpiece finding stones on his postal route and carrying them back in his pocket, or, as the stones got bigger, hauling them in a basket or a wheelbarrow. He worked at night by the light of a kerosene lamp mortaring the stones of his hymn to nature in place and subjecting himself to the ridicule of his neighbors who

saw him as eccentric.

The result is a mixture as unusual as the stones themselves. It looks like a castle of poured sand although the stones were "as hard as pebbles." He saw himself as the servant of this project, not its creator. It was "a sculpture so strange that it is impossible for man to imitate." The surface of this completely useless building is almost giddy with intricate rock shapes piled this way and that. It seems to waver in the sky like a layered cake stacked too high, and yet, as the shadows of evening form around it, *Le Palais Idéal* takes on the solemnity of a Hindu temple.

~ ~ ~

I don't know what it is about baking in a beach chair with eyes shaded that is conducive to thought, but it works for me. Maybe it is all that blinding radiance that leads to creativity or being shaded from radiance by a pulled down ball cap that carves out a secret place for the mind to work. It might be the concentric circles of stitching in the bill—the happy symmetry of it all—that lets the mind expand outward toward a new thought shimmering at the brim, the rings culminating in a kind of event horizon that sucks away all the heaviness of life, allowing nothing but abstractions to glimmer at the margins.

"À la source de la vie j'ai puisé mon genie."

I pulled the cap down lower and sank back further in my plastic chair. That's when, in a moment of inspiration, the sand castle fortress formed completely in an airy shimmer before my half-closed eyes. It would have two parts of equal importance and size, a sand castle with a palace for the unicorn and a courtyard with a fortified garrison for protection of the castle. We would start tomorrow morning after high tide, searching for a strip of sand that is perfect for packing before filling our buckets and sand molds to shape the outer walls. Working all day with the kids' help until it is done, we would watch the construction—a blueprint abstraction that expands with increasing complexity under my ball cap bill—spread across our section of Folly resplendent in the morning sun. Beach walkers would have to step around the sprawling compound which we could admire up close on the beach or in its full bilateral glory from on high in the Crow's Nest.

Building the fort would get Owen to leave the beach house behind and come down to the sand and play, and it would encourage Maddie to do more than jump the waves all day. I doubted that it would interest Anna who relentlessly attacks the beach and Caroline would pay it no mind, but the big kids might play together at that wonder spot where water meets land. Of course, the fort is doomed. The walls that grow strong and hard in the sun as the sand dries would only last until the tide came in, sweeping away our day's labors, but for the "each" of this particular god of a day it would do. I crossed my arms over my t-shirt and smiled, my lips in line with the concentric circles on the hat bill.

Yes, for a day it would do.

~ ~ ~

In the beach house before lunch Maddie studies the digital picture frame that Angie and I load with pictures as the week goes on. Maddie holds the frame in both hands, looking into, not at, the screen, as if it hid a secret. When it switches to the next image, she clicks it back, tilting her head to take in the message of the photograph. When she has finished, she puts the screen down and skips off to the Dinosaur Room to play.

Like Maddie, the screen moves on again.

I put down my things and walk across the room for a better look, clicking the screen to get it back to her picture. It shows her in the carport on a porch swing with the other kids. Owen looks a little subdued in his superman muscle shirt and blue swimsuit, one hand draped nonchalantly from the arm. He looks directly at the camera with big, dark eyes as if to say "We done here?" Anna is the animated one, leaning forward to the camera, her mouth open, caught mid-word. She wears a white top trimmed in lace and a red skirt with yellow piping, and the camera has her straight on so that the pink soles of her flip flops show up boldly. Whatever she is saying she is saying loudly. Caroline is on Maddie's lap in the center of the swing, and looks as if she is about to slide off, her pudgy legs forming a cup, her toes just below Maddie's knees. She frowns, holds out one hand as if to grab Anna's hair, and looks off at nothing apparently, lost to the moment.

Despite the commotion, Maddie commands the scene. She looks very pretty, her face caught in an expression of surprise with her eyebrows slightly raised and her mouth open in a smile. Her thick, curly, chestnut hair, loosely pulled back, glows like a halo, backlit from the beach glare. She gazes off to the side meaningfully, not blankly like the baby cousin in her lap, as if she has caught the eye of someone next to me— the me taking the picture and the me looking at it through her eyes. She is looking past both versions of me.

The picture freezes the children in a moment, but the screen moves on to the next image.

The screen wants to move on.

I push it back.

In the picture Maddie's eyebrows arch expectantly and the eyes fill with curiosity. Was it this look in the eye that held her attention as she stopped in front of the digital frame and lifted it in her hand? This look of wonder at what's ahead. Of getting ahead of herself. Of looking past me into the future?

The screen moves on, following the arrow of time.

~　~　~

Nessa, Maddie, and I come from a long line of bad dreamers. My grandmother talked in her sleep and at the end of her life lived in constant fear whether she was awake or asleep. I have bad dreams too with elaborate narratives of people and monsters transforming themselves in stories with unpredictable but surprisingly right endings, but since they begin in some pre-verbal part of my mind, I have trouble putting them into words the next day. All I can talk about are bits of the tale.

"The deck chairs were in the shape of toadstools," I explain to Barbara while we are drinking morning coffee. "And the top of the toadstools were sawed off."

She looks at me puzzled.

"That's it. That's all I've got."

I also sleepwalk. When I was a boy, my dad found me one time in the neighbor's yard wandering around in my pajamas and carefully walked me back to the bedroom without waking me. I have no memory of the event. When Matt was about to graduate from high school I dreamed that I was addressing a class of graduates in long robes, and at a dramatic point in my speech I lay my hands on the podium and leaned forward only to wake up and find my fingers wrapped around the porch railing of my house. I was talking to a line of trees in the woods across the street.

Sleepwalking and night terrors are both classified as parasomnias, Maddie and I sharing different versions of the same nightmare.

~   ~   ~

Electricity is funny matter. Like fire, it is both matter and energy. When it runs through a wire it acts more like matter since the charged electrons are material, but when it is an electromagnetic field—a billowing of attractions and repulsions--it acts more like energy, and it is this energy field that I imagine when I think of Wikipedia, an invisible, substance-less cloud enveloping the earth. Electricity is the *wiki*—the quick, flashy nothing—where the *pedia* of learning lives.

Wikipedia as I use it is a synecdoche for the whole cache of ideas and languages that exists virtually in cyberspace. A castle in a kingdom of castles amid countless kingdoms all stored in the cloud. Sometimes I picture it to be an actual cloud—one of those towering cumulous beauties with a dark head and a glowing and flashing underbelly that lumbers across the sky darkening and drenching all in its path, but filling its space occasionally with glorious flashes of illumination.

At other times I imagine cyberspace to be a nearly invisible grid wrapping up the globe in its mesh of interconnected lines, each line a path and each node on the webbing a handful of choices, an elaborate seine lowered onto the globe that contains what we know, and some of the nodes—such as the ones around London, New York, or Hong Kong—are nearly black with their crisscrossing while others, like the lines that race across the ocean before me now, thin out and seem to disappear.

Sometimes when I look into the night sky, I think of Wikipedia. An ever-expanding digital rendering of human knowledge, it is, like the universe, an explosion held in check by the gravity of its contents, a glorious spume of words approaching but never reaching an end.

Sometimes I think of it as the thought of the world, and thought, of course, is funny matter too, invisible but luminous with borrowed light.

~ ~ ~

"Why is it called Folly Beach, Owen?" He stops and gazes up to the right for a moment, thinking, and smiles. He's got it.

He points past the rickety underpinnings of the walkway to the steps leading down to the beach sand. "So many steps to go low to the beach."

We both look at the stair treads silhouetted against the bright sand.

"Fall-y Beach," he says pushing both hands down as if he were closing a trunk.

~ ~ ~

Black is back. It lands on its customary crow's nest perch, ruffles and settles feathers, assumes an elegant shape against the sky, and glares at me. It is the "o" in "silhouette," a figure hunched against filmy white clouds, wing feathers cutting irregular notches out of the sky and clouds. It is the "ouch" in "notch," the "hook" in "beak," the "ace" of spades in "space." All edges, its body, throat, and head appear to be the result of clever scissorswork. It is the "hiss" in "scissors" and the threat in the throat. It is negative space clipped out of the glare, terrifying not in its presence, which is like a wad of black construction paper glued onto pasteboard, but in its absence, the lack of color and shape and meaning at the end of the end of the boardwalk in the beginning of the middle of another perfect ending to the day. It is the "lack" in "black" and the black in lack. I can go on like this forever. It is the "ever" in "forever" and the never there as well. It is the emptiness of any tautology. The black in "black." And black is back.

~ ~ ~

The Ludicrous Library is beginning to take shape. While Nessa and Brooke poke through the pieces matching colors, I lift the box top to see what the final product will look like. It's a crazy scene in which walls are floors and floors are walls. Book cases, crammed with books rise up on the sides and line the walls and ceilings, the books hanging precariously. Stairs defy perspective turning this way and that, winding through the picture like a wave. A king, several monks, a man or woman with blue hair, some shrouded figure and a child in a brightly lit room are the patrons, but so is a bat, a beaker with bird's feet, cats, and several blue cat-like figures. The day outside of two windows looks blue and serene, but the view from a portico shows a night scene with bright stars and black birds flying through it. A chaotic abundance held within artificial and lopsided boundaries gives the structure the instability of a heap and the words on an open book run off the page and onto the desk.

The dream of every writer. The curse of every writer.

I set aside the box top and look at the real thing. A world of clear lines out of place.

The fingers of Brooke and Nessa hover above it, filling in the holes.

~ ~ ~

The kitesurfer is back too. He appears as a distant smudge on the dusky sky, but quickly is upon us as we all stand at the railing to watch. Leaping into the air and appearing to fly above the waves he grabs the tail of his board and skims the surface of the water heading out toward the horizon. Moments later, as if by magic, he reappears at the shoreline in front of our spot. Could he go in any direction despite the constant offshore wind? He seems in complete control and without limitations.

And then his hat blows off.

He makes a turn by leaping in the air again, but the cap keeps going, landing among rocks in the jetty. The surfer reaches behind to grab it, but—too late. He rides out with the wind toward the horizon and returns to the spot—maneuvering his board near the stones, looking for the cap. He performs heel turns—moving the board back and forth—to keep from sinking into the water as he holds a stationary position and leans forward, looking into the rocks, and I see that, no, he can't do *any*thing he wants. He must follow the arc that the universe provides and which he resists at some peril. It must have required great strength to hold that position at odds with wind and sea because he repeats the maneuver several times, dashing speedily toward the horizon and tacking back slowly to hover in place for a few moments looking for the hat. He can participate in beauty, but he can't control it. When he gives up, he turns his back on us, heading first toward the horizon in one more quick dash and, hatless, tacks back lazily in the direction from which he came, his kite shifting back and forth overhead, waving goodbye.

Six

WE BUILD THE FORT. I find a stretch of sand, marked off by two sunken buttresses from an old jetty that is close enough to the receding tide to be hard and smooth and with a stick make two large squares in the sand. I gather up several kinds of molds in a black-and-white toy bag. There's one for the towers and another for the walls, and one small bucket for the two large central structures: the castle keep and the Donjon. At first the kids don't notice, but Nessa, curious, comes over and starts to pack some molds.

Barbara has the walls, and I'm in charge of the corner towers. I discover by trial and error the best spot to quarry the sand. If the sand is too dry the crenellated tops of the tower simply crumble, but if it is too wet the sand sticks to the plastic when I pull the mold away. I settle on an area twenty feet away and dig there. Even with the sand just right, I have to be sure not to pack it too hard and to make repairs to the battlements after I lift away the mold.

The kids become curious. First Maddie joins us filling up a blue mold that Barbara gives her, and Barbara switches to digging a moat with a green shovel. Matt, back from his morning run, sits on one of the pilings sweating profusely and drinking water from a plastic bottle as he studies our handiwork approvingly. Owen and Angie arrive with an orange beach ball covered in white stars that he sets beside his dad so that he can help.

"What he likes to do," Angie says leaning into me, "is stomp these things down."

But he holds back seeing we are all pretty into this. He and Barbara pick out a damaged whelk to decorate his Donjon. It looks forlorn—half eaten away by tides—a fractured winding staircase into the empty sky, meant to signal doom and alarm to oncoming enemies no doubt. Owen crosses his arms and nods, pleased with the choice. He is equally pleased with the gateway of broken twigs—meant to simulate enormous posts-- that divide the two halves of the structure.

"We can just kick this in!" he shouts, making explosive sounds while pumping his arms and wearing the ominous expression of a warrior on his face, but he doesn't.

Maddie finds her own, more complete, conch shell to decorate her castle, giving it a delicate crown, and begins to find other shells for windows. Someone discovers a mold for a squid in the bottom of the toy bag and decides that it will protect Maddie's castle from within the walls to keep out any beasts who crash through Owen's defenses. Good thing too because

Barbara comes back from another shell-hunting expedition with the hollowed out carcass of a horseshoe crab, a prehistoric, ageless thing that stalks the fort from outside the moat like a dragon, a menacing carapace of doom just beyond the castle walls!

Somewhere along the way, we all stand back to look at our fortress—an impressive morning's work that unfolds before us like an open book. It is the structure that matters, a pleasing set of molded walls and buildings guarded by a squid and beset with danger from a horseshoe crab.

Of course, the crab is not the real enemy. It is just ugly and grotesque. The threat to our little world groans in the distance beyond the walls and the moat, the ocean itself, pulled away for now by the graces of the half hidden children's moon, but soon to come roaring back, when the nearest of all celestial objects dipping toward night sinks into the western sky. One of the battlements has already begun to topple, threatening the entire illusion, but I right it with my thumb.

~   ~   ~

Follies are what they aren't. In addition to their useless and extravagant nature, there is "often an element of fakery in their construction," the electronic cloud declares, and "the canonical example is the sham ruin." Great Britain is littered with these pre-crumbled piles of stone. The four-story gothic tower of the sham castle at Wimpole decked in alternating cruciform and ogive windows intentionally looks dilapidated and weathered. The gloomy Mowbray Castle in Hackfall woods is faux as well, though over time it has become the real thing—a ruin of a ruin now under reconstruction to return it to its originally ruinous state. "It seems as if every estate in England must have its counterfeit fortification," writes Barbara Jones, "complete or artfully ruined, a little bit of Olde England among the pheasant preserves."

The finest of these may be among the most lowly—the castle on the grounds of Hagley Hall, designed by Sanderson Miller and built by Sir George Lyttelton in the nineteenth century, a folly made to look like a plundered Medieval castle. It stands on a rise among beeches and other hardwoods. Fallow deer roam the grounds. The largest tower capped with merlons at the battlements stand erect and largely intact at a corner of the keep. But the rest, the crumbling walls with arched windows of fractured stone draped in ivy, create the illusion of ruin. Jones cites a contemporary source on the thoroughness of the designers: "to wipe away any suspicion of its being any otherwise than a real ruin, the large and mossy stones…lie about the different parts of the building in the utmost confusion." Even the "glossy arms" of ivy planted along the bulwark add to the illusion of antiquity, making it "impossible to look upon it without a suggestion of its being as ancient as it appears."

But a folly, a thing of appearances, *is* also exactly what it appears to be—at least the folly part is. Hollowed interiors, contemporary mortared seams, and the interior metal scaffolding must be hidden away to "keep the whole design in its purity." A replica takes the place of the real thing, rising up to stand for the aspirations of its maker as time washes it away and, in this case, mocking the passage of time in the process. These are the mossy stones, crumbling embattlements, and glossy arms of our illusions.

My first response when I picture these sham ruins is pity, followed, if I am generous, by love.

~   ~   ~

Maddie is afraid of the ceramic fish that guards the sliding doors of the beach house. It has the rough stony surface of an ancient artifact, but it is not really meant to be scary because the shape is bulbous and stylized, almost cartoonish, like a porcelain volleyball with fins and a tail. It is the mouth that frightens her, a gaping hole with wide tubular lips opening presumably to take the hook. I could easily put my hand in it.

For the first day Maddie gives it a wide berth as she heads to the beach, holding her towel to her face and rushing past without looking at it directly. It is the kind of object that prompts night terrors.

This morning she tamed her fears by feeding the beast rubber bands, one by one.

"Worms?" I ask.

"No, Grandpa," she says, as if I'm being silly. "Pasta."

She closes her eyes and nods firmly.

~ ~ ~

Matt and I are at the Crow's Nest at night after others have gone to bed. Moonlight picks up the spray of waves as they lap against the shore—dark silk gloves pouring coins from one palm to the other—while I stir my drink during a pause in our conversation.

"Waves are fractals," Matt says. He did his dissertation on orbifolds, which is a field of mathematical research based on an understanding of fractals.

"Fractals generate large systems that are uniform, but unlike a perfect sphere, if there is such a thing, they allow for wide variation."

The way he describes them, they are elusive and ever changing, falling in and out of their essential nature. "Waves cresting on the shore," he adds, pointing to the ones that are crashing just beyond the pier, "are fractals, but the horizon in the distance looks like a perfect sphere. We know that waves are varied fractal forms rising and falling—but at a distance they look completely uniform." He motions with a flat hand toward the sea. "Smooth."

Variegated and uniform at once.

Folly and its opposite.

~ ~ ~

Alfred Hall is another matter, altogether. It is a folly that has fallen into disrepair—another sham ruin made real over time—but, oddly, the feel of the pile of stones does not seem to have changed. One of the earliest sham castles, it was built by the first Earl Bathurst and Alexander Pope in the eighteenth century. It lacks the symmetrical designs and mathematical precision of Tresham's Folly—it was always a "conglomeration" to use Barbara Jones' word, the opposite of a feathery fractal design and an anachronism in the Age of Light—so the broken windows and rusting metal support scaffolding of the present-day crumbling version retains the spirit of the original.

The rounded rocks of the tower façade appear jammed together like piled skulls around a large mullioned window of stone and shattered stain glass. "The later builders of sham castles tended much more to symmetry," writes Jones who sees Alfred Hall as a throwback to an earlier time that captures "the real horrid feeling" and "the true baronial rust" of The Middle Ages.

There is charm in the hodgepodge of rubble not unlike the shapeless squalor of shells heaped among seaweed along the beach, and the sill of the gothic window, a lower lip of chiseled stone lined with boulders, has the winsomeness of a lopsided smile. I'm tempted to compare it to the Crow's Nest rising willy-nilly out of the sand on pilings and cross timbers, but the folly is not rickety enough. Asymmetry fills the eye with surprises, nooks and crannies among irregular shapes, suggesting the inherent life of the forming rather than the formed, the sprawling universe expanding into the black beyond.

~ ~ ~

Sometimes the waves sweep over me and Maddie knocking us, laughing, into the water completely and dragging us to the shore. I prefer things this way, haphazard and topsy-turvy, leaving much to chance, but I won't go as far as Michel de Montaigne, the father of this form that I write in, and simply take my ideas as I find them, trusting them because I had them. "What do I know?" he famously said, and I agree, but I feel the urge to shape my confusions according to my intuitions rather than merely record them. I want the wave, not the water, the dance as well as the dancer, the shape of the thing as well the thing itself.

My friend, the poet Kathy Winograd, says she enjoys "being pulled back and forth like the waves" as she reads my book. Another friend, the writer Bob Root, says that "one thing leads to another in a kind of prismatic effect, shifting from facet to facet, linking them through echoes and changes of focus."

"I think of fractals," the writer Sarah Einstein said over lunch one day describing my style, moving one hand in a spiral. "Each part spins off," she said spinning her other hand in an opposite spiral, "giving rise to a similar shape that takes you somewhere new." I'm not sure those were her exact words, but I am sure that her hands were spinning that way, mesmerizing hands making lovely shapes as she talked.

~ ~ ~

What I can't see from The Crow's Nest, no matter how hard I try, is what is beneath the skin of the sea: enormous canyons deeper than any on dry land hidden underwater and built—as Edward Abbey wrote in *Desert Solitaire* of the Canyonlands—according to the "the leisurely economy of nature."

"It will be good to see a lot less sky," Barbara said when we flew back from Phoenix headed toward our mountain home after gorging on the bleak beauty of the deserts of the American West where Nature takes forever to create follies that are glorious and ridiculous and poignant: Zion, The Arches, the Grand Canyon, Canyon de Chelly, and Bryce Canyon.

But here, at my feet on Folly Beach, I look out on undersea canyons far deeper that disappear below the empty horizon.

~　~　~

Matter matters—take skin. Anna's skin, the same shade as the highlights of her blonde curls, like drifting sand but smooth and gathering into dimples, those whorls that the universe loves, there like a kiss on her cheeks.

And Owen's skin set off against his dark hair with an olive glow just under the surface, more like evening sun than morning sun, a melancholy, valedictory smoothness, awaiting the press of a thumb or the cupping of hands.

And Maddie's skin, so variable and subject to her moods, rumpling above the eyes in a frown or slackening when distracted or smoothing out in delight in broad strokes like the sea spreading across sand at high tide, a giddy and impulsive swelling.

And talk about smooth! Baby Caroline's skin in the morning sun. Her mother likes to set her on her back on a blanket in the middle of the living room floor with nothing on but a diaper looking up at the world of adults and children passing by. Few can resist poking her round belly that gives like a balloon at our touch or ruffling the fuzz of red hair on her topknot. She watches, smiles, and kicks her feet.

Sam, who sees her day after day, makes a joke about how boring babies are.

"She's probably made more fresh synaptic connections in the last hour than you made all of last year," Matt says as a retort, laughing, and Sam nods.

Owen is the one who can't resist her. He told his Mom that he wanted to take Caroline home with him. He gets on the blanket and holds her fingers, runs his hand down her tummy, and lays his head beside hers. She kicks and smiles.

His skin inviting too in the morning light. Uniform. Undifferentiated. Manifold. Expectant. On the floor together they look so vulnerable, this smoothness exposed to summer light.

Later when Caroline and I are alone I come closer to look—and run my hands across all that soft. She smiles and kicks. I know that if I could zoom in, could see her skin under a microscope, it would be highly differentiated, made up of cells that fold into each other in a lumpy, epidermal design not unlike my gnarly fingers.

It would look tough, scarred, not expectant, but already there, resistant to the world's imprint.

Variegated and uniform at once—that is the miracle.

An ocean of skin.

~ ~ ~

When did Bashō's haiku about the irises on his sandals happen? That's the question I asked my students in a class during my last year as a teacher. We were working off of Sam Hamill's translation of *Narrow Road to the Interior* which is a mixture of poetry and prose called a *haibun*. My students and I could figure out from the prose section that Bashō and his friend, Sogo, arrived in the town of Sendai sometime in May of 1689. The visit lasted several days and was important because Kaemon who lived there had tracked down sites referred to in poems that Bashō and Sogo knew by heart. On the last day, the visit ended with a touching moment: before Bashō and Sogo continued without him, Kaemon gave them a map of other sites for the poets to visit on their journey as well as the sandals with blue straps.

But what is a moment? If time stretches out in one continuous line then a moment is but a dot on that line. I close my eyes and picture a clothesline and a single, glistening drop of dew. "In Bashō's best poems, each individual perception is all there is," writes the American poet and translator Robert Hass in "A Note on Translation" for *The Essential Haiku*, "and at the same time, it isn't anything at all." All and nothing. I picture the dew drop evaporating away.

But the moment is not the only time when the haiku happens. Bashō and Sogo arrived in Sendai on an annual spring holiday, "the day we tie blue iris to the eves and pray for health." The phrase "blue iris" is not only his individual perception of a moment that will vanish instantly, it is also part of a celebration that comes back year after year. The time of the poem folds back on itself, the individual moment living on at the festival each spring as people tie irises to their eaves and offer each other gifts—*and* recite this poem.

But that is not what stays in my mind as I lie on the beach hat pulled down over my eyes trying to remember the exact wording of Hamill's translation. I remember the tan cover of the quality paperback edition and the line drawing of the old poet bent over a walking stick with a sedge hat slung over his shoulder. I remember the faces of students listening as I read though I don't see individual faces, just faces. And suddenly it comes to me: "blue irises/ blooming on one's feet," an image fresh enough some three-hundred years later that I can remember it and see the poets standing beside me in the beach sand, smiling and wearing their new blue shoes for the long journey that brought them to me. The image rises out of the dewdrop of a moment, but fashioned into art it is a gem in its setting, irreducible and timeless. Bashō and Sogo head off reluctantly ducking under the shadow at my eyes with their walking sticks and disappear into the bright horizon line that forms at the end of the bill of my cap, sandal straps a-glow.

"So when does the haiku about irises on Bashō's sandals happen?" In memory, I ask the students again, but no one answers of course. I have the poem and the sandals and the dying blooms, but not the individual faces.

Just faces.

~ ~ ~

It is time to ambiguate matter. It is not immaterial that the word for matter, the stuff of the world, is the same as the word for importance, the meaning of the world. I don't want to get hysterical about this, but take, well, hair. The youthful Socrates did not think much of it in the *Parmenides,* saying that mud, dirt, and hair were so vile that they could not raise themselves to the level of meaning anything. Surely the older, balding Socrates would disagree. Consider Maddie's luscious auburn mane. Owen's handsome dark brown mop twisted with a cowlick. It has meaning to me. What can ever replace that? Caroline doesn't have much hair, I know, but I love the wispy cloud of fuzz that surrounds her round baby head. Soon that will be gone, replaced by lovely waves, I'm sure, but that spume of hair that brings a chuckle every time I think about it will be gone for good. Matter is never immaterial as in irrelevant, but, alas, it doesn't last. Anna, who looks the most like me, has a blonde flop like her mother's, but in some pictures it looks like my hair when I was a baby. I'm bald now, but when I look at childhood pictures of myself I had a blond flop too. Matter is fungible, and, when it goes onto something else, it keeps to itself and leaves us behind.

~ ~ ~

"Get your *stinky feet* out of my *face*," she says, kissing Maddie's soles and rolling with her on the rug.

Aunt Nessa knows how to make 'em laugh.

On the porch, she lets Owen and Maddie tickle her neck while sitting on her lap, Nessa laughing hysterically, head thrown back, mouth wide open, arms wide, and eyes shut into two half-moons. When Angie tries to take their picture, Nessa settles down smiling beautifully, but the kids keep laughing holding up their fingers to cover their faces, and Nessa grabs them both around their necks and holds her hand in front of her face too, and Owen is really beginning to crack up now, looking at Nessa's open-mouth laughter, both children happily undone and giddy in her arms.

~ ~ ~

Maddie cries when Owen plays vampire and sucks blood out of her stuffed penguin, tossing it on the rug and hiding a grin.

Anna cries when her Mom says, "No ma'am."

Owen cries when Maddie rides her bike too fast through the Crow's Nest.

Caroline smiles and smiles and smiles on her blanket and then cries for no reason.

After a good deal of crying Owen agrees to sit in his beach chair down by the water, and later, when his parents call him to come in for lunch, he stamps his feet in the water and cries no, no, no, no, no!

We should join them, crying too, like Maddie, Owen, Anna, and Caroline at their worst, join them in open-mouthed slobbering, sobbing, and screaming because each wave that crashes in a spray against the sand withdraws and never returns the same again. But at Folly Beach we touch them instead—make faces, pat heads, rub legs and arms, and laugh. Once, I saw Sam cut a caper, holding a wadded up Pamper at arm's length.

Barbara and I walk down the beach to get away from it all.

"One week is enough," she says squinting into the sun.

~ ~ ~

Maddie stands before me with eyes closed. An off-shore breeze blows chestnut hair away from her cheeks, the curls on both sides of her face catching sunlight and tossing it away. She is relaxed and still, arms at her side. The crimped coil of the bow on her nightgown matches the curl of her lips, and, like all of the children her skin is smooth, but here, in all this light, it looks creamy, too. Her peaked brows and crescent eyelashes encircle the swell of her closed eyes.

I stop playing.

"Why do we have eyelids, Maddie," I ask, for no particular reason.

"To keep out the sun?" I offer when she does not respond. "The water?"

She sways back and forth and smiles.

"To sleep," she says dreamily.

~ ~ ~

The fort—our folly—looks brilliant, the twin castles mighty and fortified, bounded by thick walls and topped with a cracked conch. As we gather around it our bodies cast evening shadows over the scene. With one wave the sea spills into the moat and laps up the walls. Maddie adds more shells and shifts the empty hermit crab shell into a defensive crouch guarding one of the jackknife-shell drawbridges. Squinting in the glare, Owen surveys the enemy as it swirls closer. He pats the waves with his bare hands and then cups his hands against the approaching water, but the tide floods between his feet and hands and sweeps past him. It creeps between wall crevices, disintegrating buttresses and spreading onto the castle grounds. Owen and Maddie dance in front of the tide, waving their arms and screaming at the water but they cannot stop its advance.

One corner completely collapses and water pools there and soaks into the dry sand. Maddie and Owen create an outpost for survivors on the tops of sunken pylons and throw mud inside the castle to build it up, but the water keeps coming, hitting the beach from one angle and receding in another forming foamy chevrons as it retreats, getting closer with each series of waves. Soon another corner collapses and the entire moat fills with water. A wave brings down most of the eastern wall and water in waves comes crashing into the

fortress. Unable to contain his excitement, Owen dances more wildly, arms in the air when the castle begins to collapse. He grabs some mud in both hands with no clear plan, but stops and merely stares as waves overtop the Donjon and flood the empty hermit crab shell. The castle keep is the last structure to fall, collapsing into its own melting foundation—the cupola roof sinking into the dark fortress sliding like a sash into sand lit yellow at sunset--and when it is done, Maddie and Owen stomp down the rounded remnants of former glory. When we leave, the fortress is indistinguishable from the rest of the beach as if it were only a dream.

Seven

TODAY'S SUNRISE IS an array of gray veils. I look past one of the hexagonal corners of the Crow's Nest and can make out nearly white glowing lines within the clouds forming a V shape and pointing out toward another glowing line along the horizon, but the sun is draped in lamé and there is no color here in this otherwise uniformly overcast sky.

In the mountains of Virginia this winter after three days of snow, Owen looked out of his doorway and said, "Where's the road now?" That's the kind of day we're having even though this is the beach in summer. I'm in short sleeves and swim trunks, but I feel the gloom, if not the chill, of the undifferentiated sky.

The familiar houses with darkened windows along the beach are hunkered beside their choppy breakers waiting to awaken. The exotic silhouette of the house with the cupola roof fades. The sand itself, stippled with rain from last night, has a sandpapery graininess to it. The lone jetty visible off in the distance, curves into a single parenthesis. Beyond it water and sky form an implacable colorless expanse meeting at a vague horizon.

Down, down down-up, down, down down-up, down.

Where are the crows? It seems that this would be their kind of morning when sky and water wear shades of colorlessness, but all I see is a string of pelicans making their rounds gliding along the water line. The sky pulls the sash of its robe tighter and turns away. Drops of rain hit the weather-beaten railing—one here, another there—and disappear into the cracked gray wood. I tuck the ukulele under my t-shirt and wait out the drizzle.

~ ~ ~

When the crows arrive they are pestered by rusty blackbirds that keep them from landing in the dunes where some food has fallen: oyster shells like angel wings tossed in the dirt after a party. Two crows perch at the railing near the porch waiting for the right time to try again, and one with a tumor on its head lands on the PVC pipe of the shower at the other end of the boardwalk.

Maddie points at the tumor and says nothing.

The rain has stopped, but the backdrop to the bird remains slate gray so the silhouette is clearly visible, this crow more raggedy than the others—the wings less sleek, the flight feathers rumpled. Maybe it's old. Clearly sick. The tumor nearly the size of a ping-pong ball bulges above one eye. The skin over the tumor is distended causing the feathers to go awry exposing a scaly white scalp. As the other crows extend their wings to confront the rusty blackbirds again, the sick one holds back, but beneath the ugly brow, his yellow eye watches everything. "Catch them," Maddie says, running toward the other crows and stopping at the railing.

A scuffle among the birds begins.

Maddie watches.

The sick crow watches her from his perch.

I watch him.

~   ~   ~

During the Civil War, before the battle to take Fort Wagner, the Union troops prepared the staging area on Folly Beach. They "dug a zig-zag pattern" of trenches along the northern stretch of the island, a long, narrow and winding grotto of sand and shells. They had to work around "the shallow graves of fellow soldiers" and used dead bodies of their comrades to "fortify the walls in their trenches." In the attack Union forces held the fort briefly, but were defeated the next day losing 339 soldiers.

A week later 600 black soldiers from the 54th Massachusetts Volunteer Infantry launched a second attack from Folly Beach in the first major Civil War battle by a black regiment. The regiment was outnumbered and suffered heavy casualties including the death of their commander before being driven back, but they created so much destruction that the Confederates abandoned the fort soon afterward. "Colonel Shaw and the men who fell with him were virtually canonized by the abolitionists and by a large segment of northern opinion," historian James McPherson explains in *The Struggle for Equality*, quoting from an article in *The Atlantic Monthly* at the time: "Through the cannon smoke of that black night the manhood of the colored race shines before many eyes that would not see."

In a letter to Gerrit Smith dated July 28, 1863, black journalist Angelina Weld wrote about praise for the "brave colored troops" that died at Fort Wagner coming from newspapers normally hostile to the abolitionist cause. "I have no tears to shed over their graves," she explained, "because I see that their heroism is working a great change in public opinion, forcing all men to see the sin & shame of enslaving such men."

To President Lincoln, "the use of colored troops" in battles such as Fort Wagner constituted "the heaviest blow yet dealt to the rebellion."

The National Anti-slavery Standard called the fort a "holy sepulcher."

A grotto transfigured.

~ ~ ~

"Follies are fragile," Barbara Jones writes. The owner runs out of money or has bad luck. Sometimes the architect is incompetent and the thing falls down. Most follies are vulnerable because of their distance from where the owner lives. Often hidden in among rocks or in the woods or built on a hilltop far from the main house, they are the perfect target for vandals. During World War II, citizens who escaped London along with soldiers "in the various home and allied armies" lived in follies and sometimes out of pique or discouragement demolished the unprotected structures "with venom and thoroughness." Sometimes they set them on fire for the fun of it. "There's a folly, let's pull it down," Jones writes catching their attitude. To the practical world—the world of commerce, the world that makes war—follies are an affront.

~   ~   ~

Looking back on our doomed sand fort, it is not the symmetrical shape, the two squares that opened like a book on the beach, that stands out in my mind. Nor the moat—that trench dug out around the entire structure that filled with water and acted as the first defense. Nor the sturdy bucket cylinders of sand that served as walls and barbicans holding back for a time the ocean waves. The two separate but equal interior structures were impressive, the Donjon with its hand-shaped stairway flanked by turreted guardhouses and the Castle Keep—that's what we called it—the somewhat austere living quarters for the queen with crenellated walls that sagged and crumbled a bit near the top in aristocratic disrepair.

What stays in my mind, though, was something elegant, articulated, and mysterious: the seashells. "We can decorate it with shells," Barbara suggested when I first mentioned the idea. While the rest of us were packing plastic molds with sand, Barbara carried a bucket that the kids filled with shells along the shoreline. We pressed shells into the ramparts and turrets and parapets of our sand castle. They lined sections of the outer bailey and adorned the embrasures of interior buildings. Some bedecked the drawbridge and others were tossed randomly into the moat.

Seashells lined the finest grottoes at places like Goodwood Park and Merewood, or the shell-lined water works of the Lion's Den grotto, and I remember what Barbara Jones wrote about shells which grow by accretion and borrow their beauty from the undulations of the sea itself.

The shells that best symbolized the folly of our defenses against a rising tide were the damaged conchs that topped the Donjon and the Keep. The one on the Donjon was barely half a conch, the rest having been crushed by surf and exposure. It stood, with little more than the first twist of a curve intact, suggesting the missing whorl of the whole. The one above the Keep was more complete, the damaged half of shell along the vertical revealing from top to bottom the inner chambers that wind like a staircase upward to a small, white crown, a recapitulated upward sweep borrowed from the movement of waves but more dignified somehow, exposed and frozen this way, like a pair of hands rising in supplication.

The shell on the Donjon—looking like a lost cause all along—toppled before being stomped into the mud by giddy children. But when the Keep came down, Maddie and Owen, arrested by beauty, stopped to watch as the topknot crown of the conch wavered, eventually succumbing under the blast of waves that shook the foundation. It flipped comically sideways for a moment before being swept back to where it came from.

~ ~ ~

On Christmas in 1989 snow blanketed the beach, drifted against the roots of palm trees, and sifted into the breached roof of a foundered house not far from here. In a photograph taken by Wallace Benson, the city's police chief at the time, the house appears frozen mid-fall like a frosted layer cake slowly tumbling to one side. Snow piled in the back porch in drifts that tilted toward the ocean, exposing a crack that ran halfway across the ceiling joist. The cause of the crack: Hurricane Hugo.

The rare snowstorm happened three months—almost to the day—after Hugo, the single worst natural disaster in the history of Folly Beach. Thirty years earlier in 1950, Hurricane Gracie hit the island and caused millions of dollars' worth of damage, but Hugo was worse. The storm itself was larger than the state of South Carolina when the eye passed over coastal towns with winds reaching 135 mph. Twenty-seven South Carolinians died and more than 100,000 residents were homeless. The cost climbed to 10 billion dollars statewide.

Photos taken the next day show houses washed away from their foundations and dragged into the ocean. In one photograph a row of houses leans forward like a wave and debris—lumber, cinderblock, and broken pavement—make the roads impassable. In another photo kelp is strewn along the road leading to the center of town with telephone poles leaning this way and that overhead. A boat blown up to the roadside "remains there today," Stratton Lawrence wrote, "the famous Folly Boat, which is painted on an almost-daily basis."

~ ~ ~

Sand billows and swirls around our car as Barbara and I follow a flatbed truck loaded with metal tubes. Sand sweeps across the windshield in veils and spins behind us in the rearview, a nebulous pinwheel rotating through the currents of a line of cars before drifting in skittery heaps along the side of the road. Erosion, I think, and renourishment.

Last year when we arrived on the island the ocean came up to the sand fences beside the house in high tide submerging the steps leading up to the Crow's nest. This year, after a local campaign to replenish the sand, officially called "renourishment," the beach behind our beach house has risen dramatically, above all but a few steps to the walkway, keeping the water at bay during high tide.

"I think they lost several streets from erosion once," Barbara says back at the house.

"You mean the first street was not named Arctic?" I ask, and she shrugs.

Eating a sandwich, Sam walks into the conversation during a break from the beach.

"I don't know about any lost streets," he said, "but I did read that they lose seven feet of beach a year."

Barbara and I stop at the Sands and Tides shop in town to buy Folly Beach ball caps and t-shirts, and I ask about the sand renourishment campaign. I'm upbeat, glad that the beaches are being protected this way, but the lady behind the counter, fiftyish with a dark tan and tawny, lined skin, wearing a Folly Beach visor, looks at me skeptically as she checks out my stuff.

"They did it in '92," she grumbles, squinting off toward the windows that face on a white glare. "Now we're getting half the sand at twice the price."

~ ~ ~

Owen confiscates more bookmarks and tosses the books over his shoulder. He hits a shelf of summer novels by the likes of Leon Uris and James Michener, books that get started at the beach, but rarely finished, most with small slips of paper stuck in the pages.

His uncle, Sam, as a baby used to go to sleep with a bookmark curled around his finger. In Owen's case bookmarks flutter to the floor, the confetti of our reading. A celebration of fresh starts.

Owen the bookmark bandit.

The emcee of fresh starts.

The guardian of the end.

~ ~ ~

"Crow" is not just a symbol. It's also a word. It has a sound, "krō," that is both soft and grating, the hard "k" muffled by the long "o". The mellowing is odd because the etymology—going into the past through the German *krähe* and the Old Norse *kraka* to arrive at

122

the ancient Indo-European *ger*—all refer to an ugly sound, a cackle, although *ger* is also a low growl deep in the throat. The word has an orthography, "crow," not "Crowe," "Craw," or "Kroh," common surnames associated with the word. It bears a rather dull-sounding technical definition, "a large, non-migratory corvid with a glossy black plumage and a harsh call," the Webster's dictionary on my computer explains. It settles into our grammar as a noun but can sound off as a verb for a shrill cry of triumph or pleasure. It also combines with other words. We stake "scarecrows" in our gardens and wear "crow's-feet" on our faces. In America, we "eat crow" when we are humiliated. It rhymes with "know," "slow," "beau," and "snow."

It rhymes with "foe."

~ ~ ~

Most of the horseshoe crabs tossed onto the beach are empty shells—washed clean by ocean, sand, wind, and gulls—but this afternoon some kids at the beach come across one in the breakers, dead but with much of the insides intact, and one of the teenagers grabs it by the tail and brings it in. He sets it face down in the sand, but flips it over with his toe so that we can check out the insides. "That's the mouth." I hear him say, pointing to the center of the shell, "and he eats with those claws." He taps the long, sharp telson with his toe. "It's not a stinger."

Later I learn that the claws are called chelicera—a pair of specialized appendages that define the species. The other defining feature is blue blood. Baby blue. But there is no sign of that here, I see, after the kids get bored with their catch and wander off. All I find is a tangle of sand-encrusted, segmented, body parts, some partially rotted away, all of the evolved complexity of the creature, decaying until nothing remains but the hard and lifeless exoskeleton.

A universe winding down, I think, squinting as I look up to the empty horizon.

~ ~ ~

Nessa is in the bedroom singing "Sweet Baby James" to Maddie, a song I used to sing to her. I'm standing just inside the open glass doors to the porch caught between her soprano and the churning ocean. It's dark outside, but the room has the yellow glow of a cupped hand around a lit match. The edges on sofas and doorways go soft in this light and the room itself closes in on Nessa's voice which sounds a little weary, but content after a long day of mothering.

I start to sing a low harmony in my head trying to recall those nights when I would send my kids to bed with a song, and picture myself sitting in the hallway outside their upstairs bedrooms, sitting Indian style with the guitar in my lap in an otherwise silent house, and before I realize it, I am singing in harmony along with Nessa loud enough for her to hear above the constant whoosh of the sea. It's a joke I guess, this little back and forth between us from separate rooms, and I smile but keep on singing, sending a message just to her, both of us aware as we pull the lyrics from memory that we are indulging in nostalgia.

Maddie will have none of it. She makes her mother stop. "Sweet Baby James" is their song, meant for them alone, and I'm an intruder. Maddie whines, and Nessa has to comfort her by whispering. My singing has become an excuse for another song—prolonging this lengthy bedtime ritual for Nessa even more. Chastened, I walk silently to the kitchen and open the refrigerator to fix myself a drink. When I cross back in front of their room, Nessa is singing a song that I don't know.

Eight

I'M UNDER MY BALL CAP again, gazing at the eerie half-light on the underside of the bill. This time I notice a salty, white, meandering sweat line like the foamy residue of surf on beach sand or the vague contours of the Milky Way superimposed on the concentric circles of stitching. Is this disorder, or a more subtle ordering filtering through a more obvious one? Is this order overlaying life or life seeping through the order? Or both. The area above the salt line—the top of what I can see if I roll my eyes upward under the cap—is darkened with my sweat. If I slowly shift my eyes downward, I can see the circular stitching illuminated from below by the glare creeping under the brim, a glowing, wavering horizon of my own making.

I begin thinking about time. It is all around us and nowhere. We can save it, waste it, kill it, and arrive in the nick of it, but we can't change it. We can measure time but we can't see it or touch it. We can dial it and give it a face, but we cannot turn back the hands of it. Slowly a new idea forms. A sundial! Another scheme to bring Owen down to the beach and to get Maddie out of the waves. Without removing my cap I find near my right hand a hollow reed about eight inches long. I smooth the sand with my palm and poke the stick in so that it stands upright in the sun's glare and watch it cast a shadow toward me, a gloomy finger. I picture the sundial in my mind, with a much larger center pole than this thin reed, located on the site of the flattened sand fortress. By placing stones—no, shells—at the tip of that shadow every hour, we could chart the progress of the sun across the sky, using the beach as a solar clock, marking out a clear symmetry, with the shells falling into an equally spaced circle in the sand.

"Perfect!" I think.

~ ~ ~

At night, I walk out onto the Crow's Nest alone and look at the moon against the random spray of stars in the Milky Way. Looking down at waves washing up against the shoreline, I remember sand billowing in spirals out of the tubes in the back of trucks that Barbara and I followed earlier in the day.

The futile war against erosion.

In 1878 the Army Corps of Engineers replaced the natural harbor of Charleston with jetties made of wooden pilings and riprap stone. "Cutting directly atop the sandbar that once ran from Sullivan's Island to Lighthouse inlet," Lawrence writes, "the rock obstructions claimed as much as 500 feet of shoreline from Morris Island each year." Storms did serious damage as well. In August of 2011 Hurricane Irene roared over the island sweeping "asphalt, parking spaces, and road out into the ocean."

"The wide beaches" of Folly Beach, Lawrence concludes, "may forever be a thing of the past."

The word "erode" comes from the Latin phrase *ex rodere* which means "to gnaw away" and later when I compare the aerial photographs of the island with those before the hurricane it does look as if some creature nibbled at the long stretch of sandy beach and gnawed off the southern tip.

"Once this rocky coast beneath me was a plain of sand," writes Rachel Carson in *The Edge of the Sea*, "then the sea rose and found a new shoreline. And again in some shadowy future the surf will have ground these rocks to sand and will have returned the coast to its earliest state." She imagines coastal forms that "merge and blend in a shifting, kaleidoscopic pattern in which there is no finality, no ultimate and fixed reality."

She calls it "the stream of time" with the "earth becoming fluid as the sea itself," but I see the playing out of The Big Bang. I see those tendrils of cream "reach into the coffee in intricate and beautiful ways."

Time's arrow.

Entropy—the unstoppable force—the inexorable process of temporarily increasing complexity on the long path to a lifeless equilibrium when time stops.

The creation of a glorious universe followed by its slow crumbling.

A folly.

A beach.

I set down my drink, lean over the railing of the Crow's Nest, and look down at breakers in moonlight glittering like teeth.

~ ~ ~

The Wikipedia logo—you've seen it. It's a globe of jigsaw puzzle pieces inscribed with characters for the "w" sound from languages around the world. Some of the pieces are missing at the top suggesting, as Wikipedia itself explains, "the incomplete nature of the project, the articles and languages yet to be added."

When I lift it in my mind and tilt it to look in the top, I can see an unfinished globe, but I also see a globe coming apart. All of those characters for one sound written in languages as diverse as Latin, Japanese, Armenian, Arabic, Cyrillic, Hebrew, Korean, and Thai. A globe of babble.

It looks like Danny Decapitation is back, hiding puzzle pieces of the world in his pocket.

~ ~ ~

The perfect sundial that had taken shape under the brim of my ball cap had one telling flaw which we discovered, well, in time. We got to work a little before ten. I had found a piece of broken and discarded slatting about three feet long with numbers along one side and the remains of an orange ribbon at the top that had been used as a marker in the past. Barbara and I decided to work together without much explanation. We sensed that others would become curious and join us. We went back to the spot of the old fortress which was now a flat expanse of beach with some windblown sand scuttling across it. The sun blazed in the east, so when I plunged the broken stick in the ground, a shadow line immediately formed at its base pointing back toward the beach house.

With a red plastic shovel, I cut a large circle—maybe six feet in diameter—with the stick at its center. We were done with the circle by ten o'clock and at the hour I drew a hatch mark in the sand marking the spot on our sundial. Later we placed ten small shells in a line beside the mark, identifying the time. My idea was to create a clock so that the kids could see a connection between time and the movement of the earth around the sun. When it was completed I hoped it would look like the face on my watch.

At eleven we marked the second line, this time adding eleven shells, and all seemed to go according to plan. Barbara and I built a perimeter wall with the same molds we used to make the ramparts and turreted bastions of our fortress. At twelve o'clock we chose a small conch to mark the noon spot which seemed like just the right touch. Matt joined us looking at the structure for a moment and casting an eye toward the sunny sky, and he explained what we were doing to Owen who wore a t-shirt emblazoned with a bright yellow streak of lightning. They walked the beach gathering more shells in a plastic sieve, preparing for future hours to pass.

And they did. At one o'clock we cut a line in the sand marking the shadow and Owen put one of the shells in place. He also counted the other shells with his thumb. Soon Nessa and Maddie, who were working on their own sand project, dropped by to see what we were up to. Clouds started developing overhead, but the shadow was still visible. That is when I began to notice that the clock had a mind of its own because the space between twelve and one o'clock was noticeably larger that the space between eleven and twelve. When we stood back and looked at the whole it was clear that as the day wore on the spaces between the hours were increasing so that the dial inside the circle did not look exactly like a clock, but more like a geometry problem.

Matt, the mathematician, gazed at the sand clock and then at the sun, shading his eyes, muttering "it must be the, uh…" and paused. He is not one to leap to conclusions. That did not stop me. "It must have to do with the angle," I said, sweeping my arm across the sky, but, really, I had no idea. By the time we got to two

o'clock the disparity was the largest, the space equaling the size of the entire spread between ten and one. Proud of our work, we stood beside it taking pictures as more clouds rolled in. Fortunately, it never rained and at each hour there was enough light to mark the shadow. After two, the spaces closed up, and by the time we reached six o'clock the space between five and six in the evening matched the space between ten and eleven in the morning dividing the circle in half.

We fixed a batch of Margaritas to celebrate, sitting in our beach chairs watching the sun sink according to a plan we didn't fully understand.

~ ~ ~

"Those flies *like* having a sick man around," Bashō joked on his deathbed. They were his last words. In his final years he found himself quarrelling with his students, angry that they were writing to win awards and prizes. He even thought of giving up writing himself but could not: "something always stirred my heart and mind."

Out of step with his times, he looked back to great poets who came before him, the Chinese writers Po Chü-i and Du Fu who suffered physical hardship for poetry. They were his true colleagues now that he was old and sick. Though he did not claim that he could match their talent, he believed that he and they shared a "phantom dwelling," a folly built with words.

He was fond near the end of his life of a treehouse he constructed so that he could gain a better view of the mountains. He called it his "Monkey's Perch." I suspect he would have felt at home in the Crow's Nest, too, and would have liked the pelican-level view of my phantom dwelling.

In his final hours he wrote a death poem about his dreams wandering the desolate fields, but when a friend asked about it Bashō said that all of his poems were death poems.

~   ~   ~

Wings locked, pelicans float in formation patrolling the shore. We lift our hands to shade our eyes in silent salute.

"Destroy the *Sith* we must," Owen croaks, pulling a pretend cloak around his shoulder and walking with a limp.

~   ~   ~

Since we built the sun dial, we have become more aware of time's passing—sort of. Maybe we are more aware of our lack of awareness of time while on the beach. "What time is it?" Barbara asks after she had just set the stone for eleven. When I point to the sundial, she laughs.

The sun is so bright and uniformly intense at midday that it seems to obliterate time. Sand and water and sky create in our minds a blindingly luminous landscape that wipes away hours as petty distinctions. We talk in broad strokes of an afternoon at the beach. A day at the beach. But the beach blanches the hours of the day. The waves keep a kind of rhythm, but it is so dreamy and seductive that it lulls us.

The sundial is the antidote to this beach oblivion. It robs the afternoon of its timelessness. It gives meaning to the shadows in the sand that hug every person and object under the sun's greedy gaze. It reminds us that the shadows are there and growing larger and that the earth itself—this glowing ball tipping us for now toward the light—casts an umbra deep into space, but we don't always pay attention.

Later Nessa asks the time, apparently missing my conversation with her mother, and Matt turns to her wagging his finger with mock indignation. "Don't you see the sundial right there?"

~ ~ ~

Hermann Minkowski stood at the chalkboard delivering the address "Space and Time" to the 80th Assembly of German Natural Scientists and Physicians, at Cologne, on September 21, 1908. He drew a mathematical graph on the blackboard, but had more on his mind than math. He was interested in the chalk. This "chalky axis," he said slowly drawing a line across the board, "as it is consists of molecules all athrill is taking part in earth's travels in the universe." It was a reminder to his listeners that his mathematical ideas, though they defied common sense, were not merely abstractions, but rooted in a new understanding of the physical world.

"The views of space and time which I wish to lay before you," he warned, are "radical." They have "sprung from the soil of experimental physics," and their implications are far-reaching. According to a collection of memoirs called *The Principle of Relativity* written by scientists who were there, he argued that the three dimensions of geometry—length, width, and height—are more elegantly understood when they are yoked with time. "Henceforth space by itself, and time by itself, are doomed to fade away into mere shadows, and only a kind of union between the two will preserve an independent reality." With that chalky line he stood the Newtonian world view on its head, and as the parabola he drew above the axis bent downward, he said triumphantly, "suddenly three dimensional geometry" has become "a chapter in four-dimensional physics." That chalky line described his "world postulate" which we have come to know as "Minkowski spacetime" or the space-time continuum.

He dared scientists to prove him wrong: "there will be ample suggestions for experimental verifications of the postulate," he explained, that would win over "those to whom the abandonment of old-established views is unsympathetic or painful," but he had faith in the "pre-established harmony between pure mathematics and physics," between his numbers and the molecules of chalk "athrill" on the board. Above all, he understood—and demonstrated—that the early work of his student Albert Einstein on special relativity could be better understood by placing space and time on a continuum.

Einstein, who attended the lecture, dismissed it at first as a parlor trick.

~ ~ ~

Steven Harvey

The ocean hides a host of follies. We call a bunch of herring a "siege" and a colony of jellyfish a "smack" suggesting their intimidating appearance. Siphonophores, relatives of the jellyfish, float deep in the ocean in a shifting configuration that acts like a single organism. The sea dragon looks goofy with two glowing eyes surrounded by a leafy topknot and a lower body that blends in with the algae where it hides from predators. The caption beside the sea dragon in my copy of *Ocean Planet* describes the ocean's follies this way: "Life in a watery medium has produced fantastic body forms and unusual lifestyles." Angle fish may be the most menacing of all in appearance, round like a volleyball with transparent fins, a mouth that opens nearly half its face, razor sharp, translucent teeth, and a phosphorescent, bobbed proboscis that glows in sunless ocean depths and flutters above bulbous eyes attracting prey.

But the ocean does not have a crockagator, a generic eight-foot swamp lizard that Maddie and her mom have carved out of the sand. It has a long tail, four muscular legs that seem caught in motion, a widening midsection, and a reptilian diamond-shaped head with a long snout. When the mother-daughter duo finish, they use cracked shells to make the teeth and claws and embed dark stones deep in the sand head for eyes. Nessa's sand crockagators appear to have mass and dimension because of the way they emerge out of the beach sand. They are Nessa's specialty, a trick she

learned at Stone Harbor when she was a girl from some close friends of ours. For Maddie, it is a time to have the sole attention of her mother, so the rest of us back off a little, though we do eventually come to watch and help gather shells and shape the legs. When the sand sculpture is done we walk away and the monster seems exposed, a creature caught in mid-stride that turned to sand as it tried to escape into the ocean. By late afternoon, the ocean laps closer and the trench that encircles the beast fills with water.

Eventually it slips away into the sea leaving nothing but claws and teeth behind, and soon they wash away too.

~ ~ ~

At sunset, a black cloud, glowing red on the underside, hangs above the house like mist from a cauldron, and when the rain begins, we retreat to the porch. A few heavy drops slap the boardwalk, the beach umbrellas leaning against rails, the chairs stacked against each other, and the wide aucuba leaves growing onto the porch, but soon the rain suffuses into a flat, soft sound that surrounds us as we settle into plastic porch chairs and talk in the shadows. The sky is clear behind us in the west and the only light is a fiery glow, like candlelight. Our voices emerge low, intimate, and desultory in the semi-dark.

Nessa discusses her theory of teaching which she calls the art of inattention, a kind of selective attention apparently which means, if I understand correctly, that she has learned to address problems she can solve and ignore others beyond her control, her voice resigned but sure and confident, even hopeful, the voice of experience. We see lightning flash in the distance, off at sea, silent against the steady beat of waves. After a pause, some other voice in the gloom mentions that a soccer player bit his opponent in the World Cup that day. There's another glow in the sky along the horizon, like a lit match held up to a face in the clouds. Another pause. We reminisce about past trips to the beach and somehow get to the perennial topic of Danny Decapitation leading Matt to make a joke by sticking his head out beyond the porch rail, stretching his neck.

A crack of lightning.

A double thunder clap rocks the porch.

Matt ducks. Everyone jumps and bursts out laughing as it rumbles overhead.

~ ~ ~

Crow on the PVC pipe looking out toward the ocean.

Crow as bird ruffling its feathers.

Crow as caw echoing in Maddie's inner ear.

Crow as night carved out of the day.

Crow as a symbol, waiting.

~ ~ ~

Maddie hasn't spoken to me all morning since I told her not to smush the bread on her sandwich. When I talk to her or look at her she puts on a pout, shakes her head, and folds her arms, refusing to speak.

I'm also a little down because Owen has learned to use his pronouns correctly. For a year or so he was stuck in the objective case. "Her is getting in trouble," he used to say. Or, "her is my friend." And the rest of us would share those knowing adult looks. Now the nominative case has asserted itself—agency is established—and the link between actor and acted upon is all too clear. Guilt and shame will surely follow.

I talk with Barbara about these things as we walk down the beach to get away for a while. We step through the waves past a line of handicapped bathers sunning in wheel chairs, one complaining while the others try to calm him down.

We see some teenagers fishing at the cut—one of them lifting a large catch in the air—but when we get closer we see it is a baby shark: gill slits and wide-set eyes and a scale-less, slate black back. The boy lifts it by the tail higher for us to see, the body twisting in a torque like the curl of shells in our sand clock.

The negatives pile up: a rainy morning, too much to drink, hurt where none was intended, intentional hurt, a cough passed from one of us to another and another, a mesh of ills.

The kids create a grave for sea creatures in the sand. A melodramatic Maddie, pretending to be upset, carries a dead crab ceremoniously at arm's length on an orange Frisbee, the larger claw dangling lifelessly over the plastic lip, burial in the sea-animal graveyard the only option. She and Anna try one more time to revive it with water. "Maddie," someone says, "you tried everything"—a line right out of the script of a soap opera.

Barbara turns to me, lifts her sunglasses and cocks one eye: "CPR?"

A week *is* long enough.

~ ~ ~

A week at the beach: a folly with a built-in grotto.

~ ~ ~

"The grotto below looks just south," wrote John Aubrey in *Brief Lives*, "so that when it artificially raineth, upon the turning of a cock, you are entertained with a rainebowe." Aubrey, a seventeenth century antiquary and natural philosopher, was visiting the house of Thomas Bushell, admiring the water display at the entrance of his friend's grotto. Beneath the rainbow, a wooden statue of Neptune aimed his trident "at a duck which perpetually turned round with him, and a spaniel swimming after her which was pretty, but long since spoyled."

It was a pretty illusion, but it is not the whole story.

Naomi Miller argues that leaving the vault of the grotto is not a return to the "outside world of nature" but to the "enclosed orbit" of "the inner world of man." Seekers, groping through the receding darkness of tunnels grayed by dust and spider webs, escape inevitably the purer dark of the inner chambers of one reality only to re-engage its dusky version at another level, their terror replaced by melancholy.

The downstairs doorway stands between them.

~ ~ ~

Alexander Pope, the most elegant of the English poets, famous for his wit in verse and his charm at gatherings, knew all about the melancholy of the grotto. He suffered a body that Joshua Reynolds described as "very humpbacked and deformed." At public events in his house at Twickenham his voice was "naturally musical" and his manner "delicate, easy, and engaging," but to attend these parties he had to be strapped in bodices made of stiff canvas by a manservant in order to stand erect and as he chatted socially the muscles in his cheek tightened in pain "like small cords."

He wrote his poetry in his famous grotto on the property at Twickenham which contained a camera obscura that faced on the river and cast an upside-down scene of people in society that the writer satirized in countless couplets.

Inevitably in the grotto the gloomy side of the scribe for the *Siècle des Lumières* emerged. Constrained by humor and geniality in public, Pope could vent under the transformative influence of his private "Cave of Spleen." "Unnumbered throngs on every side are seen," wrote Pope in *The Rape of the Lock* as he studied topsy-turvy figures of passers-by at Twickenham in the sooty mirrored image of the wall at his back: "bodies changed to various forms by Spleen." He had fantastic visions of teapots with "one arm held out" and a pipkin walking "like Homer's tripod." A jar "sighs," a "goose pie talks," men "prove with child" under the influence of "powerful fancy," and "maids turned bottles, call aloud for corks." A "constant vapor" overhangs this dismal mental state, "phantoms rising as the mists arise." He saw the nightmarish faces of "glaring fiends" and "snakes on rolling spires" in a land of maladies where "each new nightdress gives a new disease."

"What do these images tell us about the creative imagination?" I asked my students. Pope usually rolled around in December in the course, and I remembered once teaching him in my now tattered, ribbed, blue cotton sweater in an old brick building where my college teaching career began as snow took the field and filled the corners of my windowpanes. I no longer remember my student's answers to my question or my responses to them, but I think, now, I know what these images tell us about Pope's creativity.

Out of his grotto he constructed a folly.

~ ~ ~

When the sun comes out, a crow settles down at the end of the boardwalk at Folly Beach with a flutter of wings. A grotto under the rainebowe of my sky.

~ ~ ~

The name Wikipedia is a portmanteau word. It comes from combining the Greek word for education "paideia" with the Hawaiian word "wiki" which means "quick, fast, swift" and is often doubled—"wiki wiki"— to mean very fast. Of course, I think of the Hawaiian phrase "tricky wiky wackies woo" from "Ukulele Lady" which gives the word "wiki" a new twist. "Waki" is related to the word "uaki" and can mean "watchful" in Hawaiian. Wikiwakipedia: a quick and watchful education—I like that. And there are a number of Hawaiian words similar to "wiki" suggestive of love-making: "wihi" for wink, "wili" for writhe, and "wi'u" for entangle. It is true that "tricky wiki wackies woo" is just a novelty phrase, a smash up of several languages created for a silly song, but Arthur Collins and Byron G. Harlan—the "Half-ton Duo"—defined the phrase "yacki hacki wicki wacki woo" as "love in Honolu" in their 1916 Edison Diamond Disk recording which I can hear on YouTube.

Yacki-hacki-wiki-wacki-woopedia. A word folly for a quick and watchful love of learning how to love in Honolulu. I can strum along to that.

~ ~ ~

Naomi Miller writes that the grotto "constitutes an elusive art form" because it can "be viewed in a myriad of contexts—sacred and profane, idyllic and bucolic, mythological and oracular, theatrical and ornamental." Individual shells may gleam pleasantly in their geometrical shapes, but the accumulation of them in half-light flickers lambently like a scaly hide and cloys. The grotto can be a site for lectures, for displaying art, or for lying in repose like the ancient Romans to feast on grapes and meat and wine. Visitors come for solitude or company. Muses and nymphs hide in its nooks and niches or sun themselves in lit alcoves. Above all, argues Miller, the grotto is "a metaphor for the cosmos," and in this it is like a folly, an example of art "imitating and surpassing nature."

Even as she writes that the grotto is nature "cultivated and controlled," though, Miller offers a caveat that separates these man-made caves from follies: they are part of the earth. The classical grotto is "so closely related to the natural source or spring as to be at one with it." Streams ripple and cataracts roar through its chambers and rocks overhead drip in its echoey depths. At some depth, insects take over, spiders draping crevices with gauzy webs, and in the cold and dank core walls decorated with shells and trinkets seep and crumble, and rot sets in. Follies rise genially from a solid, human-made, foundation, separating themselves from the natural world, but the grotto is a compromise with the planet, its shimmering walls carved from cold, wet dirt and buried in an absolute and inhuman darkness.

Nine

WHY DO I SIT at the same spot each morning—this seat on the bench in the southwest corner of the Crow's Nest, facing the northeast? With each vista splendid, why not sit somewhere else along the octagonal bench? Is it an intuitive longing for symmetry, a word that goes back to the ancient Greek *summatria*. Fond of likenesses, Plato put the word in the mouth of Socrates who in the Timaeus calls the sphere *kallistos*, the "most beautiful" of shapes because of the myriad ways it "can be made similar to itself."

But my view each morning is not made up of likenesses. It is instead a balance of opposites. The shoreline cuts a diagonal across the scene. Above the line and off to the right Venus and the crescent moon dominate the predawn sky, and those celestial objects are set apart from the area below the diagonal which is dark creating a sense of anticipation as the umbral shadow thins and objects emerge: hummocks of sand, seaweed at the waterline, a far jetty slowly take shape. Cutting across the diagonal is the tower with the cupola roof. As I watch I'm in awe of the emerging beauty. I think of Leopardi's "sublime contrast between the infinite and indefinite." In fact, the Greek word *summatria* that Socrates used did not mean symmetry in the strict sense of mirrored equivalence, not yet. In his time the word meant "proportional" or "commensurate." It is "measured," the highest of goods according to Socrates in the *Philebus*, and that is what draws me to this spot on the bench.

A measured beauty.

Kallistros summatria.

~ ~ ~

"I like to splash, crash, jump up," Maddie shouts breathlessly, leaping and waving her arms like a cheerleader with each verb. We are together again for sunrise at the Crow's Nest on our last full day at the beach. Low lying gray clouds bunch up in the sky tumbling away from the shore, and on the far horizon I can just make out dark eyelashes of rain curling away from the land weeping I assume at our departure as the last of the storm heads out to sea. I have asked Maddie why she likes hopping waves.

"To get wet," she answers, twirling around a little hysterically. "To get my swimsuit wet."

Wave hopping is the opposite of night terrors. Maddie takes each unpredictable but inevitable blast from the sea with her eyelids wide open, filling her eyes with light. She is fully awake, and only awake, unable to dwell on darkness or fear or monsters that are all safely hidden under the undulating blanket of the ocean. She is too busy laughing and screaming and coming up for air to be afraid when she is hopping waves. It is splash and cold and tingle and sun. It leaves her breathless and giddy and alive to the moment.

Wave hopping is her folly.

A rip appears in the overcast sky. Then another. Here the sun comes, and Maddie dances off imagining herself in the water.

~ ~ ~

Bolas were originally used as weapons for capturing cattle and game, and, according to Syed Ramsey in *Tools of War: History of Weapons in Ancient Times*, the Inuits used them to hunt flying birds, "fouling them in air." It is the over-end motion, usually in the opposite direction of their forward motion that mesmerizes me, a slow, retrograde spin, moving ahead by turning back. A *Kallistros summatria*. It brings to mind the flickering motion of old movies, the bodies gesturing through a series of jerky stills. The arms of the bola—because that is what they look like, two extended spindly arms—flail as it flies, replacing accuracy with a wide embrace, like some desperate parent scooping up a rescued child.

Matt had the best shot in ladder ball. It was on our third day and he had been practicing, but there was more luck than skill to this one. He held one ball of the bola in his hand and let the other ball swing back and forth like a pendulum. When he got ready to make the shot he allowed the pendulum to float backwards a little further, pursed his lips, used his arm to add momentum as the ball swung forward, and with a backward flip of his wrist and a splaying of his fingers released the slowly spinning bola to flip end over end toward the ladder. When it hit, the shot wrapped around the top bar, winding and unwinding with such force that it slipped off and snagged on the second bar, which set the bola spinning in the opposite direction, catching and wrapping around the lowest bar for the most points. It looked like a rattler slipping through a snake handler's arms. When it was finished Matt and I both stepped back, astonished.

Nessa had the worst shot. It flew from her hand and went straight up in the air. She and her mother had to run, covering their heads.

~ ~ ~

We call Aunt Alice on the speaker phone and Maddie tells her about the fort. "There were bad guys and good guys," she says breathlessly, "and what knocked the castle down was water."

Owen interrupts, saying that he stomped the castle down, and begins walking around the room like a dinosaur, taking giant steps.

Alice cannot be with us this year because she has started a new job as a counselor in Atlanta and has not accrued enough vacation time.

So Barbara takes the phone and describes the fortress as a castle keep and a donjon with a moat that went all the way around it.

"The prisoner was an Octopus," she added, stifling a laugh.

"Oh," says Alice.

"Then the tide came in and took it all."

"Tides will do that," Alice says with a sigh, sounding very adult and knowing and far away.

"And I stomped the castle down," Owen repeats, still stomping through the living room as if Alice could see.

"We can build a new one," Barbara explained, smiling.

~ ~ ~

Last year, Alice was the summer surprise. We had arranged the trip to Folly while she was a student in a summer internship program and were told that she was the only one of our children who could not make it to the first Folly Beach trip. Alice loved her program and we knew that she needed to stay.

We had a wonderful week that first summer at Folly with Maddie and Owen old enough to play together. It was there that Maddie fell in love with jumping in the waves for the first time. Barbara and I had resigned ourselves to the fact that Alice could not come.

I remember one glorious afternoon in our final days at the beach that year. I sat on the back porch with a cocktail in hand talking to Sam, both of us looking over the ocean. We watched a band of clouds turn gold and extend all the way to the horizon, giving our skin a coppery cast in the early evening light.

"It doesn't get much better than this," I said, lifting the drink in a small toast.

And then Alice walked in and it did.

She turned the corner on the steps leading up the porch, leaning her suitcase against a railing. I was floored. I had no idea. Wearing a mango sun dress, she lifted the sunglasses off of her eyes, tucking the temples back into her hair, and gave me a kiss on the cheek.

"Surprise, Papa!"

~ ~ ~

The universe is indicative--what was, what is, and what will be—but I live in the subjunctive mood, my mind iffing about like a puppy. If Alice arrives we will buy an ice-cream cake. So, once Alice arrives, the wish is our command. Oh yes, I am emphatic in the subjunctive. Alice and ice cream *and* cake. Forget the downstairs doorway! All that is possible hides in the word *if,* the premise of all folly.

~ ~ ~

I lean back and study the polished conch on display on the wall. "We are not contained within an invisible, rigid infrastructure," writes Carlo Rovelli, describing our place in the universe, "we are immersed in a gigantic, flexible snail shell." The polished coral surfaces undulate as the shell twists on itself, and I imagine planets dropped into its wide opening curving into orbit around the shell's core, all straight lines flexing into a spiral shape in a universe that has no interest in rigidity and expresses itself in swelling waves and castaway shells. "The sun bends space around itself," Rovelli explains, and planets "circle around the sun, and things fall, because space curves." They fall *away*, are drawn away, not down which means nothing in the universe. "But it isn't only space that curves; time does too," Rovelli adds, "and the unbounded extensions of interstellar space ripple and sway like the surface of the sea."

The downstairs vanishes taking the doorway with it.

~ ~ ~

"It's about time," I say, pouring out the remains of my coffee, grabbing my stuff, and heading down to the beach to set another stone in our sundial. "Time stops for no man," I add facetiously, chin up and looking ridiculous, an adventurer wearing crocks, swim trunks, a t-shirt, and a ball cap that says "Folly."

"It's about time" is an interesting phrase, I think, as I set my plastic shovel, molds, and a small bucket of stones in the sand and stand amid the glory of ocean, sand, and the opaque, flawlessly blue dome of the sky while counting down the seconds on my watch.

~ ~ ~

"Waves are made by mermaid's tails," Maddie says matter-of-factly as we wait together for the next big one. "Like this." She illustrates her theory by waving her hand in the streaked water between waves, creating wavelets.

Holding her other hand, I turn to look behind me at the slow cresting of a wave headed our way, and picture it, just as she says: a small circle of undulating mermaids deep in the ocean beyond our sight rise and dip in and out of the water like dolphins, their long fins setting still waters in motion, generating waves that gather power as they roll toward shore, some crashing on top of a little girl and her grandfather.

In Maddie's universe fear yields to the imagination.

"Here comes a big one," I shout, turning my back on a wave cresting in foam at full height. Maddie is no longer angry with me for scolding her about smushing her bread. Holding onto my hand with both hands now, she squeals when I tell her to watch out for the next one. She looks quickly behind her whipping her long, wet hair, shrieking at the wall of water, and ducks as the wave bomb crashes down on us.

~ ~ ~

The kitesurfer returns, gliding in like a corsair under the black wing of his sail. Wearing a black wet suit, he maneuvers across the white caps, his board slapping water, and at times powered by the wind and waves lifts into the air, held aloft momentarily by the arc that beauty has carved out for him.

~ ~ ~

Do words as matter matter? Probably not, but I miss the bite of words that I committed on the page in my youth when I wrote poetry on a gun-metal gray Royal typewriter that looked like a tank. Sometimes the periods and commas poked through the paper, and a vague impression of all my words wrapped in overlays around the platen, the story of my life embossed on a rubber roller. Typing on it meant business and required strength and resolve, an early and daily reminder that the task is not for the fainthearted.

I have one book at home printed in letterpress that creates the same sense of words pounded into the page. It is *Parley's Every Day Book* written by Peter Parley and published in 1834—a gift from a friend. The book contains stories, poetry, fables, and aphorisms meant to fill in the chinks in the day with bits of wisdom—those stray moments which we fill these days by checking our phones. "I have devised this little volume, for the purpose of saving these waste moments," Peter Parley explains, "and I respectfully beg the reader to appropriate them to the following use." When I look closely at the "u" in use, I can see that the letter is sunk into the pillow of the page, and when I run my finger over the word "introduction," all in caps at the top of the page, I can feel the word at my fingertips.

Letterpress uses blocks of lead type or dies stained with ink, which are pressed onto the page with grippers, embedding the letters into the paper, but each evolution of the making of books has reduced that tactile sense of words. Offset printing paints a negative image of the page on a rubber colored roller and transfers it to the page without pressing it in and, when done, the page is smooth to the touch. Digital printing uses toner rather than ink and on a computer screen the words are disembodied and ephemeral lines in light. When I touch the screen I feel nothing of the words at all but a barely perceived, flickering cool. On an iPad the words float under my fingers matterlessly as I turn electronic pages, with no loss of meaning at all.

No loss?

"When you read on paper you can sense with your fingers a pile of pages on the left growing, and shrinking on the right," writes Anne Mangen, a lead researcher with Norway's Stavanger University, who documented some loss when words leave the page, particularly in "emotional responses" to stories. What is lost is that sense of a book passing through a reader's days in much the same way as an ocean wave spills over Maddie at the beach: This movement through the physical pages of a book—the gradual "unfolding of paper"—is "some kind of sensory offload" that enhances "the reader's sense of unfolding and progress" through the story. Owen gathers book marks with one hand and drops books over his shoulder onto the floor with the other demonstrating an apparent disdain for printed words which he can't yet read, wiping out that sense of a wave of progress through the text because he cannot yet experience it himself.

Matter matters?

I'm not so sure. One day, Owen will get to books, but right now he likes screens. I remember, when personal computers first became common, being fascinated with the old dot matrix letters that rose out of the gloom and glowed magically against a green screen. Emptiness flooded through them like water. Even now, I love the way a digital word on a screen appears to hover—offset—above the world it describes. Like spume. Like breath that surrounds the words we speak. Like spirit. Printed words hammer us; digital words whisper our names in the dark.

~ ~ ~

I lean back on the sofa holding a poker hand of a dozen or so bookmarks that Owen tossed. I've lost my place in my own book. Beach, folly, ukulele. Crow, night terrors, pelicans in a long, low, undulating row. I hide a jigsaw piece in my pocket and—*boom!*—it replicates itself over and over, spinning in a fractal formation creating fresh folly out of what's missing. I follow a progression up the neck of the ukulele and, when the frets disappear, pause a moment and continue, shaping chords silently on the air. And when I write I build follies out of love and during the night they collapse before my rapidly-moving eyes, but at dawn the next day I begin to build them up all over again. My Harveypedia.

~ ~ ~

Last summer Owen let go of his Ninja Turtle kite. It spiraled into the sky, the blue tail clapping in circles around the spinning blue sail emblazoned with the face of the turtle named Leonardo, and Owen started to cry. Without hesitating Matt and Sam took off, the soles of their feet kicking back sand as they dashed across the beach, jumped dunes, and side-stepped sand fences chasing the fluttering triangle of plastic.

Barbara, Angie, and I hung back, comforting Owen who was more surprised and scared than angry or hurt. The wind had whipped up causing him to step back and let go of the reel.

About five minutes later, Matt trotted back to us kite in hand, Sam running beside him. Both were gearing up for a marathon in Charlotte that fall and were hardly winded. When Matt knelt down to his boy offering him the prize, Owen looked down and gave his dad and then his uncle a hug and ran off, leaving the kite with the blue tail behind.

~ ~ ~

Montaigne considered himself to be an "accidental philosopher." He suspected that anyone who simply recorded his thoughts as they occurred to him would eventually stumble onto some sort of philosophical insight. For him, the essay was more down-to-earth than the abstractions of philosophers. He liked to play with his cat. Like most of the French of his day, he used knives and fingers rather than forks. I think he was on to something. For me, the essayist is not a philosopher in the sense of a thinker who isolates truths from their context and applies them to all people at all times, an ocean wave wiping the beach clean of all but broken bivalves at the barren high-water mark. Essays come in wave after wave, changing the shoreline with each pounding of the surf. They are not the gleaming silverware of the mind, but a finger dipped in honey, the knife pinning a shrimp, a fingernail slipped under the shell. An essay uncovers the truth in the story by showing how the writer got there. In life, not in thought. For now, not forever. No essay has the last word.

~ ~ ~

I'll write my folly today and save the last word for tomorrow.

~ ~ ~

Like most nests, the Crow's Nest is not grounded but suspended in air, high above a tangle of bay hops, yucca, and prickly pear in the back yard of our beach rental, and is the haunt of birds as well as Harveys. When we gather here in the early morning for coffee before the sun gets hot and in the evening for drinks, huddling together, we look out far beyond our small circle to the wide horizon.

I read in *Bird Nests and Construction Behaviour* by Mike Hansell that there are only two ways to build a nest: "sculpting and assembly."

Grotto and folly.

Assembled from lumber and sculpted out of the boardwalk, the Crow's Nest simultaneously satisfies contrary urges, the desire to be hemmed in by a small and enclosed structure as we gaze far off and dream.

~ ~ ~

I pull up a chair beside Nessa who has been alone on the porch watching sea gulls hovering in the offshore breezes.

"They make it look so easy," she says, tilting her head without taking her eyes off of the birds.

~ ~ ~

The Swallow's Nest folly overlooks the Cape of Ai-Todor on the Black Sea. The stone castle itself is tiny, a *châteaux fantastique* a little over sixty feet long perched high on the Aurora Cliff with a clear view of the sea and the distant shoreline of Yalta. The original structure was a wooden cottage with white trim, nicknamed the Castle of Love, but in 1911 Baron von Steingel tore it down and built the current folly in its place.

Despite the stone walls and the rugged setting on a rocky ledge, the building does not look austere. There is a childlike silliness to its ornate spires so that from a distance it looks more like a sand than a rock castle. Perched precariously above the waves like a ship's prow, it at one time nearly tumbled into the sea. In 1927 an earthquake with a magnitude between 6 and 7 on the Richter scale rocked the building, which, I read in Wikipedia, was undamaged "apart from some small decorative items that were thrown into sea along with a small portion of the cliff." The promontory developed a "huge crack: and the castle was closed for more than forty years until restoration began in 1968.

It is aptly named—the Swallow's Nest—clinging to the rock like those mud cups that swallows build in caves and on the underside of outcroppings, but Castle of Love still works for me as a name for a sequence of boxy, white chambers topped with an assortment of turrets and flag-tipped towers reaching hesitantly from a pile of rocks into the blue Crimean sky. It waits on its cracked ledge, laid bare to all around it, with the vulnerability of an exposed wrist held at arm's length, and a coziness of scale mixes with its gradual upward movement suggesting human yearning like cupped hands held out for water.

~ ~ ~

Barbara and I are on the porch setting out ham sandwiches for lunch. Right now the water is blue-green and calm with a single fishing boat in a middle distance between the horizon and the shore, a focal point in a wide and empty beauty. She winces when she sits down.

"You all right?"

"Except for my back"

"Except for your back, you're all right? Having a good time?"

"Yes I *am*!" she announces, sitting back. "And you?"

"You know me." I smile and tip my hat back with my drink. "I'm having the time of my life."

Having the time of my life is an interesting phrase. How do we have it, really? Do we spend it or keep it or pack it away in memories. Does life slow down when we're having the time of it? Or speed up? Does it glow like a sundial on the beach? Does it glower like a sand fortress?

Or, does it darken with long shadows as evening sets in. There is always a sore back or busted toe or heart lurking about during the times of our lives. A bone growing brittle and waiting to crack. A swelling we don't feel ready to burst and taking as long, we like to say, as it takes.

Life fills when I'm having the time of it, but when I am having *a* time with it, time flattens like a wide expanse of empty beach and ocean and sky with me bobbing somewhere in the middle distance. The sundial made of sand slowly fills with water as the tide rolls in and the laughing children, who know nothing much yet about time's passing, take their own sweet time as a birthright and stomp the crumbling towers flat. It all happens in the time we are, one way or the other, having, and in the fullness of time the ocean swirls in behind and sweeps us all away.

~ ~ ~

When I was Owen's age I could flip a bicycle onto its seat, spin the wheels, and watch the glittering spokes appear to roll first forward and then, as I spun the wheels harder, slowly move backward in a retrograde illusion called temporal aliasing. In between—when the spokes seem suspended in a quivering standstill—time appears to stop. This is childhood time, Owen's flexible time, when a summer afternoon extends forever.

I like the phrase "time dilation," the word "dilate" coming from the Latin for extend, but when broken down by syllables—*dis* for "apart" and *lâtus* for "wide"—the etymology suggests an opening and swelling of time. Eyes dilate, the iris thinning around the widening black pool of the pupil. So does the cervix at birth. The ventricle dilates in cardiomyopathy when the heart enlarges.

So does time. Differences in gravity and velocity alter time, so a clock on a satellite in orbit goes more slowly than one on the ground. At the beach we measure time with shells: the shadow of the stick on our solar clock moving slowly in the morning speeds up in the afternoon, so that the spacing between the shells is uneven, the arc ballooning outward. "Dilatory," I think, remembering widening spaces on the solar clock as the day wore on. Does time lose much of its meaning in retirement, in a world without deadlines?

No, there is always a dead line.

~ ~ ~

When I first started teaching, I read the *Duino Elegies* by Rainer Maria Rilke on my back stoop in

Charlotte, North Carolina. It was the Alfred Poulin translation. Burgers cooked on the grill and the willow tree at the end of the fenced-in yard shuddered in the breeze as I turned the pages. But it was not until my last year as a professor some forty years later that I finally got around to teaching the elegies for the first time. The students were a plucky bunch and soldiered through the writing of daily annotations as they read, but it was spring and the text seemed inscrutable to them, and I found myself waiting out long pauses in class.

"So why are we here with our language and our consciousness?" I asked walking among the desks with book in hand, stopping to lean against the windowsill at the side of the room. It's the Rilke question. It's *my* question. "What does the poet mean when he says that our task is to 'resurrect the earth in us invisibly'?" The students copied the phrase, which I had written on the board, and stared at the words in silence. Afternoon light poured in through the glass, adding a honey-like glow to the room.

In the poem, a wanderer on his way to die brings nothing physical with him. All he has are his words, the poet's words, plain words like "*house, bridge, well, gate, jug, olive tree,*" I say reading aloud from the book. And "*window*" nodding toward the wall of windows beside me. Maybe "*pillar*" and "*tower.*" Plain words. "These are words that the wanderer has earned," I explained, "they glow, italicized, in his mind, and 'the things themselves never dreamed of existing so intensely.'" The light shimmered in their silence and my mind went back, for some reason, to the willow wavering in the breeze in

Charlotte as smoke from the grill poured down the hill and floated through the branches nearly forty years earlier. Lost in reverie, I barely noticed how quiet the room had become.

"It's like virtual reality," one student finally ventured, breaking the silence and bringing me back. "The world out there and another world of computer simulations."

"Okay," I say happily, wondering aloud what Rilke would have thought of virtual reality headsets or the gauzy alternate reality of cyberspace that seems to envelop the planet. None of the students laughed.

"But he's talking about words," one of them said. Words once pounded out on my old Royal typewriter, I thought, vanishing now into digital thin air.

"Well, it could be any kind of art I suppose, but Rilke had in mind words." The magic is in the transforming power of the words, what the words create in each of us. "In the introduction to your book," I say, taking a moment to flip back to the page, "Mark Doty calls it the 'transformative, preserving word.'" The willow branches in the smoke looked like shadows, I remember, when I closed the book that evening in Charlotte and just gazed into their apparitional shapelessness. "As the world itself vanishes before your eyes," I explained to the last class I would teach at the college, "words recreate it in us. They preserve it in us."

I pushed off from the windowsill, my shadow flitting across young faces as the sun got lower in the sky, and walked to the front of the class. "'Earth, isn't this what you want: to resurrect/ in us invisibly,'" I recited underlining the phrase on the board. "Isn't it your dream/ to be invisible one day? Earth! Invisible!"

~ ~ ~

Last year Alice and I swam out past the breakers. All week I had stood right at the breaker line with Maddie, being pummeled by waves, but Maddie was playing in the sand and I liked swimming with Alice into the calmer waters where the waves swell but do not crash and the water lifts us. Slowly we drifted apart—I was closer to the jetty of stones that fingers its way out into the sea—and I felt the ocean pulling me at an angle that would take me near the rocks. I called to Alice, but I'm not sure she heard.

"Go back," I shouted. "Back!"

Whether she heard me or not, she started swimming back to the shore before the water could pull her deeper in.

I tried to get to the rocks. I know that's dangerous—these rocks can scrape and batter you, you cannot get a footing on them, and the scratches and cuts take forever to heal—but I couldn't help it, the pull of the water out to sea was too strong and I was afraid of where it would take me. I did catch one rock, just below the surface with my hand and tried to pull myself up on the stones above the water, but the undertow was too strong, and I was yanked from the rocks to continue my slow, but inexorable, drift out to sea.

By this time the family saw what was happening and they gathered on the shore, waving.

I saw Sam—the strongest of us—start to head into the water but I waved with both arms for him not to enter. I think he saw me because he decided to follow my drift parallel along the shore as the water carried me past the jetty. Sam crossed the jetty on the sand and got a nasty cut on his foot on the sharp rocks there but reached the other side, tracking my journey.

For a while I tried to resist the waves, to crawl back to the breakers again, but the current was far too strong for my arms, and I slid down the flexing muscle of water, my efforts puny. I decided to conserve my energy and drift. Go with the flow, I thought, already exhausted and breathing hard. Looking down the beach I saw the skyline of rooftops and realized that I was headed for the house with the cupola roof, and the window, lit yellow at dawn, now dark.

That's where we're all headed, I thought.

The moment I gave in and rode with the sea, the panic subsided, and I felt calm. I yielded myself—no, gave myself—to what I would one day become, and fear and anxiety did not rise in me; they dissipated. The sun felt warm on my face, and, with the water as my guide, I rode the current past the jetty and drifted outward.

Yield and overpower. Yield and overpower.

And that's when the sea let go.

I felt it instantly as I crossed the jetty line.

I'm not sure how much truth you can get out of an essay. No matter how long it is, uncertainties pile up. Descartes defended clear and distinct ideas when he wrote his book-length essay, *The Meditations*, but he was shaken by doubt, most of his life. Certainties he claimed one day turned brittle the next. He described his despair as a terrifying and constant state of near drowning: "The Meditation of yesterday has filled my mind with so many doubts that it is no longer in my power to forget them," he writes in the F. E. Sutcliffe translation. "I can neither put my feet firmly down on the bottom nor swim to keep myself on the surface."

The essay is the doubter's Bible. You ride it or drown.

I waited until I was completely past the jetty and started swimming as hard as I could back toward my family who had all crossed the jetty by now and were watching me swim in. I saw a surfer wading into the water toward me carrying his board. He's going to help me in, I thought, but as I found my footing in the waves crashing around me, he dipped his board in the water and smiled.

"Looks like fun," he shouted, and began to paddle past me, into the waves.

~ ~ ~

Talk about folly! Our beach neighbors, who have been drinking all afternoon, decide to take the catamaran out to sea at dusk. Six of them—three men and three women—are sitting in plastic chairs in a semi-circle around a cooler, talking to each other animatedly, shading their eyes, and pointing toward the horizon. The more they drink the louder they talk and the harder they laugh. The boat leans beside them in the sand.

Suddenly the men leap up and drag the double-hulled craft down to the water.

They raise the mast, the pastel panels looking somber in the evening light as they lift the boom and adjust the gooseneck. Two of the men help as the women, off balance, climb on board, stepping carefully around snap lines and taking seats on either side of the mainsail.

One of the women places what looks like a six-pack on the canvas, and the two men, hip-deep in water, wait on a receding wave. The water is pretty choppy, the jib flapping loose in the wind, and when the men shove off, the masthead tips precariously leeward and a cheer goes up as one of the men secures the boom and the other, unsteady on his feet, wraps his arm around the mast and draws the jib taut.

The arc of sail against sky forms.

Silly. Dangerous. Beautiful.

Eventually the crew right the craft and, clearing the breakers, head off toward the horizon, several of them saluting each other with raised beer cans against a dusky sky as one woman leans back and nonchalantly drags her hand beside her in the foam.

Ten

ZENO WAS A STUBBORN MAN. In a story told by Diogenes Laërtius, he died because of his involvement in a plot to overthrow the ruler of Elea. When hauled before the tyrant and asked to name his other conspirators, Zeno requested permission to approach and whisper the names. When the tyrant leaned closer, Zeno bit his ear and would not let go until he was stabbed to death by guards.

He was clearly wrong about his paradox. The number of points between Zeno and the knife may be infinite but they are on a completed line. What lies between the tyrant and the philosopher is a continuum, not an endless series of points. We bite the ear to reach an end.

But what end?

~   ~   ~

Philosophy begins in wonder, Plato said in the *Theaetetus*, and Aristotle in the *Metaphysics* agreed, filling the world with hope, but that was long ago. Now we have follies. Maybe it's enough.

Those who seek beauty should begin with the human form, a woman named Diotima of Mantinea told Socrates in the *Symposium*, but, as they grow more mature in their thinking, that sense of human beauty should expand to include all physical objects—"the limitless ocean of beauty" in the Michael Joyce translation. Eventually, though, the true philosopher can shed the need for the physical—for matter—completely, can leave the teeming ocean behind, and see the beauty of ideas themselves. It is an appreciation of a beauty beyond nature that is "eternal, neither coming to be nor passing away, neither increasing nor decreasing. Moreover, it is not beautiful in part and ugly in part, nor is it beautiful at one time, and not at another." It "exists for all time, by itself and with itself, unique."

For me such disembodied beauty is the vanishing point, half again and half again and half again away, forever out of reach. Oh, I see the *kallistos summatria* of the ocean and all that passes away, but permanent beauty—no. That first morning at Folly, the shoreline formed a diagonal against the horizon at dawn, cutting a wedge of black ocean between sand and air as I unpacked my ukulele in the Crow's Nest. Venus and a sliver of moon rose above a cloudbank, and, while I checked my tuning, waves beat against sand in the half-light like slow and heavy breathing, and I saw the house with a cupola roof and a single window lit yellow against the dawn. Oh, it was beautiful and the world seemed to stop, but only seemed to. A moment later the window went dark and the sunrise dimmed.

"Gaze upon the limitless ocean of beauty," Diotima told Socrates, the physical world one step away from the Platonic ideal.

It is as close as I will ever get.

~ ~ ~

Near the center of the Parc Jean-Jacques Rousseau stands the Temple to Modern Philosophy. The structure was inspired by the famous French writer

and philosopher who spent the last six months of his life there, the bucolic setting restoring his love of nature. "For a long time, my heart drew me here," he told his friend René de Girardin who had inherited the land, "and what my eyes see make me want to stay here always." When he died on July 4, 1778, he was buried at midnight on a small island on the property, the way lit by flickering torches.

To honor the writer, Girardin built the park according to a principle he described as "joignant l'agréable à l'utile," joining the pleasant with the useful, and its centerpiece, The Temple to Modern Philosophy, has a similarly lofty principle in its design, being left unfinished as a way of demonstrating that the enterprise of philosophical enquiry is a dynamic process. When I look at the full screen photograph of the sylvan temple in Wikipedia, though, that ideal of philosophy as a modern and on-going process is lost in rubble. Doric columns support a ruined stone entablature and the frieze above the entrances are decorated with Latin inscriptions as well as the names of long dead philosophers. Mossy steps lead to the faux pedestal and the grounds are strewn with weathered boulders whitened with lichen. In this bosky park decorated with architectural fabrications, including a grotto to the Naiads, the unfinished Temple to Modern Philosophy may be pastoral, endearing, and "agréable," but it is not "util." It is, as it should be, a folly.

~ ~ ~

First, the crockagator collapsed. As the tide swept in, Owen and Maddie watched a wave take a bite out of its snout and before long the entire sand creature was washed out to sea where it belonged.

We turned our attention to the sundial which was a little further from the shoreline. While the crockagator was being devoured, I placed six shells in a row along the shadow of the sundial, marking its last hour, and waited for the incoming tide. We had built a moat around the perimeter of the dial, just as we had done with the fort. In fact the sundial looked much like a fort with sand walls, towers, and turrets forming a line of defense against time's passing, a doomed fortress made out of time.

One wave filled most of the moat with churning water that oozed through cracks in the wall, and soaked the lower end of the clock face. At a quarter after six, evening clouds closed ranks, and I feared that the clock might go dark before it collapsed. But the clouds retreated to the far horizon and the waves advanced.

Owen and Maddie began their crazy antics, running around the sundial and occasionally leaping into the air in mock fury and delight. Sunlight slid under the clouds giving the entire beach a sepia tinge illuminating the salient where several towers collapsed. At that we released the kids who switched sides and joined the assault stomping the sundial flat and scattering the shells. Owen yanked on the stake, the prize at the heart of the hours of the day, and lifted it over his head like a scimitar as darkness fell and long waves washed through pilings and swarmed over the ruin leaving nothing in its wake. We celebrated with margaritas in red plastic cups. Even Angie, who does not drink much, grabbed one as Barbara and Matt brought them down to the beach.

"What the hell," she said, saluting the end of time.

I looked in the distance.

A sunrise there, I saw, casts a sunset here.

~   ~   ~

These pelicans in formation, clouds billowing behind them, are they coming or going? Their arrival and leave-taking look about the same.

~   ~   ~

"Since there exists in this four dimensional structure no longer any sections which represent 'now' objectively," Albert Einstein wrote near the end of his career, "the concepts of happening and becoming are indeed not completely suspended, but yet complicated."

He was thinking about the geometry Hermann Minkowski first demonstrated at a chalkboard in Cologne which explains the substance of reality as a space-time continuum where everything happens at once with no room for *now* and *then*. "It appears therefore more natural," Einstein added, "to think of physical reality as a four dimensional existence, instead of, as hitherto, the evolution of a three dimensional existence."

The sense of *now* evolving into *then*, he believed, is only apparent. He had long before come around to Minkowski's view of the relativity of space and time which he used in his General Theory in 1915.

When his friend Michele Besso died in 1955, Einstein in a letter consoled the family: "for us physicists believe the separation between past, present, and future is only an illusion, although a convincing one."

~ ~ ~

The silhouette does not darken the picture; it completes it.

~ ~ ~

"In a world without purpose all is folly," I write in my little book.

"In a world of folly we create all purpose," I write, trying to get it perfect.

"In a world we create, all folly is purpose."

When I close the book the ink smudges.

~ ~ ~

When he wrote the letter consoling the family of his dead friend, Einstein admitted that our everyday concept of time is never "completely suspended," and the woe that drives us weeping to our knees is very real. We *feel* irrevocable loss as now slips away, seemingly sweeping up all in its wake, the "convincing" implacability of the illusion of time's passing being the hook on which we twist.

So I build a sundial in the sand to trace the turning of the planet, marking its hourly rotation with seashells on the oblique, but the arrow of time goes straight through me.

~ ~ ~

"It's the last day," Nessa says, an evening sunset spreading out behind her as we sit in the Crow's Nest sipping drinks. The sun has fallen just below the roofline of one of the neighboring houses, and the refracted beams shoot into the sky, shatter in the clouds, and fall like colored rain behind her.

The rain of light may just be falling in the lenses of my glasses—I can't tell.

"You think we would be getting ready to get out of here, tomorrow" she says leaning back and looking over her shoulder, her face glowing. "But it's *the last day.*"

~ ~ ~

We do not complete the puzzle. I see islands the shade of the laminated wood table top poking through the stairwells, bookshelves, open windows, nooks and crannies, and oddly shaped doorways of the Ludicrous Library and see maybe a hundred to a hundred and fifty knobby unattached pieces scattered around the margins of an impossible world. The crazy construction of stairs leading nowhere and windows each with scenes of different weather and times of day seem even more unstable in this partially completed world. Books that are floating up explode into nothingness. A stone encased doorway meant to be locked shut gapes, not open but empty. The librarian has her head firmly in place, but bodiless stares with bulging eyes at the desolation below. The largest lacuna runs through the center of the scene along the bottom of a stairway that must have been easy to fill in and crosses stacks of books to a casement made of multicolored drawers, a blank streak like a void in the Milky Way.

It is unusual for this crowd not to finish, but the Ludicrous Library was a challenge. I watch Nessa lift entire sections and lay them gently in the box, chunks of an implausible world. It is a quixotic attempt to keep the preposterous intact, but the layers of interlocking pieces crumble in her fingertips as bits of the absurd world fall away. "Oh no," she says and laughs. In a puzzling universe we make puzzles we cannot finish and stack them in the closet with other puzzles that come apart at our touch. She lowers the lid onto the box of shattered library parts and holding the remains of a ludicrous world at arm's length leaves the room, glancing over her shoulder at the floor behind the table to be sure that a piece—the key to making a future folly whole—is not hiding under the skirt of a sofa or leg of a chair.

After all, Danny D. may be lurking there as well.

~ ~ ~

On the last evening I usually try to get away and watch the ocean breakers alone. I'm not alone, of course. All along the shore others have done the same, standing up to their ankles in the water to gaze. It is not sentimentality that draws me here—I know I'm not saying goodbye to the ocean or anything like that. It's forever I'm thinking about. Limitlessness.

Matt calls the waves fractals, each alike in form but changing in scale as the crest rises toward the shoreline, and that monotonous shapeliness is part of their allure.

But here, as the sky darkens, it is the play of light on the belly of the wave, a kind of golden smear, that holds my attention, some gift of the wave and sunlight squandered on sand and rocks and me.

"Yet, if those forever dead were waking an image/ in us," Rilke wrote in his final elegy, "they might point to catkins/ hanging from the empty hazels."

Sure, they might, I think, recalling the drooping of catkins in the park where I walk at home.

Or they might point to these breakers tumbling on the shore.

"And we, who have always thought of joy/ as *rising*," the poet added, interpreting the lesson that the dead pass on to us, "would feel the emotion/ that almost amazes us/ when a happy thing *falls*."

~ ~ ~

"And the Lord says," I think, as I strum the ukulele on the last morning, but there are no slanting beams of golden sunlight pouring out of the sky this time, just a gray cloud cover with a bluish cast.

Down and down and down.

The last dawn. Within hours we will disperse, each family off to a different destination, and I'm waiting to see what this drab dawn has to say about it.

The sky behind the clouds is not uniformly gray, I see as I keep looking. A pearly light forms subtly along three lines: two diagonals pointing inward from above like a mother's arms covered in flour reaching down, powdering the horizon line white.

I play a few chords, as the ocean shimmers.

A last sunrise had better be enough.

~ ~ ~

Bashō wrote a three-line haiku celebrating hundreds of islands covered in pines visible from the coast of Matsushima.

> Matsushima ya
> ah Matsushima ya
> Matsushima ya.

To explain this poem I told my students about an impromptu poem that Barbara created during our trip to Rome. After the twelve hour flight we wandered the streets near our hotel trying to stay awake, and when we turned the corner of the Altare della Patria we suddenly saw, in the middle of the modern city, the ruins of the ancient Roman forum stretched out below us in all of its toppled glory.

"Wow." Barbara said taking in the vista, "oh wow. Wow.'

~ ~ ~

In a world of loss, creativity is the best revenge.

~ ~ ~

Confucius looked at a river and said, "Maybe letting go is like this."

What did he mean? I used to believe that the teacher's words were about resigning myself to loss and death, living in the shadows of those damned pelicans rippling across my pages, and they are, but they are also about the play of sunlight on water, right? And the melodic laughter of water on rocks, and the rhythmical lapping of waves at an old man's feet?

~ ~ ~

A woman walks down to the shore in a robe, her black terrier scampering behind her. The rising sun has just gone behind a cloud and the implacable, oatmeal gray has set in once again. She stops at the water's edge and slowly lifts both arms above her head assuming a Yoga position, though it may be Tai Chi because she leans to the left like a dancer, her movements fluid. Two children—a blonde girl and a dark-headed boy in t-shirts and shorts run from her house and join her, lining up at her side. In unison, they do their movements, mimicking her motions, beginning with a deep bow and hands raised as if in prayer just as she has done.

Worlds face off, three small bodies addressing the ocean and sky as equals.

~ ~ ~

Thresholds are a way of coming and going, and waving goodbye or hello look the same. I cross a wet line into the ocean that spreads like rumpled covers before me and leave my world behind. None of that, I know, will matter to me one day, and Zeno's Paradox will not slow me down. The arrow of time is fixed. The light under the door that closes behind me, the ukulele and the dark hole of the ukulele under my fingers, clocks and castles in sand, children and jokes, my little book and ludicrous library, Sweet Baby James, skin and hair and eyelids, the puzzle and the missing piece of the puzzle, and those voices, laughter and whispers and sobbing softened and muffled that I float beyond, and those colors, yes, all those sunrise colors, shaded by the brim of my cap. When mattering no longer matters, the sum of my folly will vanish in the glittering temporal aliasing of fading memory.

~ ~ ~

Creativity is the last revenge.

~ ~ ~

"Are you trying to kiss the Ocean, Owen," Angie asks, squinting into her camera while taking his picture at the shore line. Owen is spread out at our feet lowering his face to the water as the wavelets along the water's rim glide to him. I look up away from the two of them past the breakers to the heaving back of the wide sea and the pristine blue sky streaked here and there with clouds.

I see the silver-lined curl of a wave close in a zipper of foam and reach for my pen, but it isn't there.

It is time to bring my word folly to an end.

~ ~ ~

Barbara and I close up the house after everyone leaves, making sure that our absence is complete: dishes cleaned and put away, beds stripped, pillows returned to sofas, and the refrigerator empty. We arrange the chairs on the deck just as they were before we moved them closer toward each other. We replace the toys that littered the Dinosaur Room with a display of shells too delicate for children and rename the room the foyer. I take a photograph of one of Anna's pointillist drawings—well, really just a bunch of different colored dots—before whisking the original into a black trash bag.

We have one final ritual: coffee on the porch before we leave. I carry my steaming travel mug out to the deck while Barbara cleans the pot—our last chore of erasure—and shoo away the crows around the Crow's Nest one last time. I hear the ocean's endless roll as it wipes clear the beach of all our attempts to freeze time. When I lean over to brush sand from the seat, I feel a presence at my shoulder—the sudden strong warmth of late morning at the beach—and tilting back the rim of my hat turn to face the sun already high in the sky as Barbara walks toward me, no longer young but looking radiant in the yellow glow, her mug in hand.

And somewhere behind me a single window lit yellow in a house with the cupola roof goes dark.

~   ~   ~

"Grandpa, would you please take us to the downstairs doorway tomorrow?"

"He means soon," his mother explained. "He may mean *any* time."

Yesterday is soon. Tomorrow is any time. And what about today?

I didn't get to it until late in the week. Owen and I walked together down the narrow stairs after he finished breakfast. Who knows what demons we dispelled? I remember unbuckling the child's safety lock on the expandable wooden gate. I let him go first, his small hand reaching up to the railing that I grabbed from above. Maybe the downstairs doorway is a portal where up equals down and everything that disappears can be found? Where now goes poof into next. Maybe the invisible world is kept in storage here, behind the downstairs doorway. Maybe like a poem the downstairs doorway leads to the place where nothing is lost.

The gateway to our folly.

When we reached the bottom, I maneuvered him past the cabinet with the decorative paddleboards, the oriental fan, the bricks, the rattan hanging and the water colors all casually arranged, and opened the door slowly for him to see, hoping for something magnificent, but it was just the carport with a porch swing, shower, real paddleboards, our cars, and large trash cans. Nothing special. Owen nodded as if he already knew that. I remember he shrugged as I closed the downstairs doorway and said, "Thank you Grandpa," with that little sidelong lowering of the eyes away that he does when he is being polite.

I can see it now as if it were tomorrow.

Acknowledgements

To Jan Shoemaker, Kathryn Winograd, and Robert Root who supported me when I needed it most, to Joe Mackall who is always there for me, to my students who kept literature alive for me, to the gang at the phantom dwelling where I spend most of my time, and finally to Barbara and our family who, as these pages reveal, are often on my mind and always in my heart.

A Note from the Author

I hope you have enjoyed *Folly Beach* and will spread the word. Also, please check out the study guide that follows for questions by me designed to enrich your reading of the book.

If you would like to learn more I urge you to visit the Post-Script Press website. It contains color photos from the text, an amplified study guide, and a brief essay by me about writing the book including comments on the book-length essay.

www.Postscriptpress.com

I would also urge you to contact me through my author's website. You can learn more about my work there and let me know your thoughts about the book as well.

www.steven-harvey-author.com

Author's Study Guide: for Readers, Discussion Groups, Teachers, and Students

When asking these questions, I prefer to use the word "author" rather than "speaker" to describe the voice in the book because I believe that the authorial voice in the personal essay speaks directly to the reader in an intimate way unique to the genre. You might begin your discussion with that idea. What relationship does the author establish with the reader in the first few pages?

1. In what way is the ukulele both a blessing and a curse to the author? Why is he fascinated by the myriad possibilities for chord and rhythmic combinations? What does the description of the ukulele as a "tightly wound boundlessness" (8) mean?

2. Read the section that begins *"What's the matter, Maddie?"* (2). Is the author ever really comfortable with waving goodbye? If so, explain. If not, and he doesn't shed his awareness of mortality completely, what compensations does he find by the end of the book?

3. How would you characterize each of the grandchildren: Maddie, Owen, Anna, and Caroline? What does the description of the picture of them on the digital photo screen (83) tell us about the author's feelings toward them? (The picture is reproduced at the beginning of the book.)

4. *Folly Beach* is haunted by animals. What do the crow, the pelicans, and the various sea creatures teach the author? Are they nemeses? In what ways are they guides?

5. Read the passage beginning "Brooke lowers the strap" (77). Why is skin so important to the author? The author also insists throughout *Folly Beach* that "Matter matters" (101). Why?

6. Why follies? What do they say about those who build them? What do they mean to the rest of us? What does building a sand fort and a sundial, which are like follies, teach the author? He calls his book "my folly" (173). In what way is that true?

7. See the passage beginning "Secretly, I love Wikipedia" (22). In what way is Wikipedia a folly? Why does he love it? Why secretly?

8. Consider the writers the author taught in his final classes—Bashō, in particular. What do they continue to teach him in retirement? What is the "phantom dwelling" (127) he shares with them? In what way is *Folly Beach* a "phantom dwelling" as well?

9. Based on his confusion about the sundial, the author clearly does not have an in-depth understanding of physics, and yet the idea of the "space-time continuum" fascinates him. Why? What solace does it bring to this time-haunted book? What does Albert Einstein mean when he writes that the "future is only an illusion, although

a convincing one" (167)? Why is this balm, as presented in the anecdote about the death of his friend Michele Besso, never enough?

10. Xeno's paradox and Eddington's "arrow of time" (173) are presented as being at odds. What is the tension? Is it ever resolved? (Hint: the arrow wins).

11. The writer Sarah Einstein compares the recursive style of the author to fractals since "each part spins off giving rise to a similar shape that takes you somewhere new." Robert Root describes it as a "prismatic effect" that shifts "from facet to facet, linking them through echoes and changes of focus." Kathy Winograd likens the style to "being pulled back and forth like the waves" (100). What do each of these metaphors say? What do they have in common? How would you characterize the style?

12. When the author looks at waves in the last chapter he thinks of Rilke's lines from the *Duino Elegies*: "And we, who have always thought of joy/ as rising/would feel the emotion/ that almost amazes us/ when a happy thing falls" (171). What surprising insight about death do these lines offer? What do they say about *Folly Beach*?

13. The author finally does take Owen to the downstairs doorway and sees his grandson smile politely with a sidelong glance. What does he mean when he writes "I can see it now as if it were tomorrow" (176)?

Photo Credits

The photos of the beach and family are from the author's personal collection. The credits for the photographs of the follies and grottoes are listed below in the order they appear in the text. I am grateful to these photographers for their excellent work and to Creative Commons for making images available to writers.

1. Gene Selkov, Dunmore Pineapple, CC-SA 2.0, Source: www.flickr.com/photos/selkovjr/8546804792

2. West Wycombe Park. Temple of Apollo. Giano and English Wikipedia, Public Domain, Source: https://en.wikipedia.org/wiki/West_Wycombe_ Park#/media/File:West_wycome_Temple.JPG

3. Triangular Lodge, Rushton, Northhamptonshire by Amanda Slater CC-SA 2.0. Source: https://www.flickr.com/photos/pikerslanefarm/ 28996761841/in/photolist-LbkZ4F-Li7vxX- Li92pZ-Kmwx16-Kmhp2j-L8Qm13-Lbo77K- LfezcL-Li8t8p-KmxpxP-LbmqRT-L8QJ9b- KRNC31-KmeJKJ-Li8BMi-KRQ29Q-KmfhAs- KmeZxu-L8MYh7-L8MGJo-Kmfxyd

4. Facteur Cheval - Pierre d achoppement CC BY- SA 4.0. Source: https://en.wikipedia.org/wiki/Ferdinand_Cheval #/media/File:Facteur_Cheval_- _Pierre_d_achoppement.jpg

5. Palais_facteur_Cheval_5- Ideal Palace, Xavier Devroey CC-SA 2.0. Source:

https://www.flickr.com/photos/misterdi/340528
4524/in/photolist-6bUYs9-aXgH6Z-dSe7xk-
bdPNJT-7hyPtH-8haZn4-im25gH-3UnfGA-
6LyuwM-7Z7khu-6u6VuD-55zX1a-cm9o1u-
6BHtQ3-6bQRVv-t2JeK-55xWdv-6bQQL8-
dcPD7r-6bUZeW-6bUXpb-6bV1sQ-6bUWr5-
6bUXV7-55zYBG-d1XeKE-55AszJ-6LMm

6. Alfred's Hall, Stuart Wilding CC-SA 2.0. Source:
http://www.geograph.org.uk/photo/457253
7. Pope's grotto, Verdurin. CC-SA 2.0. Source:
https://www.flickr.com/photos/verdurin/18812
890149
8. The Swallow's Nest Castle near Gaspra, A Savin.
CC-SA 3.0. Source:
https://commons.wikimedia.org/wiki/File:Crime
a_South_Coast_04-
14_img10_Gaspra_Swallows_Nest.jpg
9. The Temple of Philosophy, Parisette CC-SA 3.0.
Source:
https://commons.wikimedia.org/wiki/File:Erm1
1.JPG
10. The Temple of Philosophy (detail), Parisette CC-
SA 3.0. Source:
https://commons.wikimedia.org/wiki/File:Erm1
1.JPG?

About the Author

Steven Harvey is the author of *The Book of Knowledge and Wonder*, a memoir about coming to terms with the suicide of his mother published by Ovenbird Books as part of the "Judith Kitchen Select" series. He is also the author of three books of personal essays. *A Geometry of Lilies, Lost in Translation*, and *Bound for Shady Grove* and edited an anthology of essays written by men on middle age called *In a Dark Wood*. Two of his essays have been selected for *The Best American Essays*: "The Book of Knowledge" in 2013 and "The Other Steve Harvey" in 2018. Over the years, fifteen of his essays have been recognized as notable by that series as well, and he was twice honored as a finalist in the Associated Writing Program's nonfiction contest. He is a professor emeritus of English and creative writing at Young Harris College, a founding faculty member in the Ashland University MFA program in creative writing, a contributing editor for *River Teeth* magazine, and the creator of The Humble Essayist, a website designed to promote literary nonfiction. He lives with his wife in the north Georgia mountains where he sings and plays banjo, guitar, and ukulele in the group Butternut Creek and Friends. You can learn more about Steve and his work at his web site: www.steven-harvey-author.com.

Made in the USA
Monee, IL
10 April 2021